FIVEFOLD MINISTRY: ACCESS GRANTED

BY

BRIAN D. BEVERLY II

Fivefold Ministry: Access Granted

Published by Outpour Press
P.O. 4014
Hammond, LA 70404

Copyright © 2020 Brian D. Beverly II

ISBN-13: 978-0-578-63093-9

All rights reserved. No part of this publication may be reproduced, stored in a retrieval system or transmitted in any form or by any means electronic, mechanical, photocopying, recording or otherwise without the proper written permission of the publisher and the author.

All scripture was taken from THE HOLY BIBLE, NEW INTERNATIONAL VERSION®, NIV® Copyright © 1973, 1978, 1984, 2011 by Biblica, Inc.® Used by permission. All rights reserved worldwide.

Any Internet addresses (websites, blogs, etc.) is offered as a resource, and is not representative of a relationship or imply an endorsement from the publisher or author. Nor does it vouch for the content associated with said references.

Printed in the USA

Edited by Amanda Beverly

DEDICATION

For my wife Amanda, who has been one of my greatest inspirations. You are the love of my life and I am eternally grateful for you.

For my children, Kamden, Ada, Bailey, and Micaiah. You are God's gifts to me and your mother.

For the Church of the Lord Jesus Christ! May the Church continue to push back the darkness.

CONTENTS

(Each chapter builds upon another. Please read each chapter in order starting with the introduction)

Introduction		1
Chapter 1	Defining The Fivefold	5
Chapter 2	Opponents Of Fivefold Ministry	19
Chapter 3	Which Office Is The Best	29
Chapter 4	Which Office Is The Best Part Two	37
Chapter 5	Becoming A Fivefold Minister	49
Chapter 6	The Apostle	61
Chapter 7	The Prophet	75
Chapter 8	The Evangelist	87
Chapter 9	The Pastor	97
Chapter 10	The Teacher	105
Chapter 11	Applying The Fivefold To Your Context	115
Chapter 12	Applying The Fivefold To Your Context Part Two	123
Acknowledgments		135

INTRODUCTION

There was a point in my Christian experience where I was not satisfied with the current church climate that was around me. I was grateful for the church and I loved Jesus Christ as I do today. However, I would leave church longing for more than what was. I would think to myself, "There has to be more than just sitting down, listening to a sermon, joining a small group, participating in humanitarian aid, and giving to God's work financially." This is not to say that those endeavors are not good and necessary. No, there is great meaning and joy from those events and God calls us to participate in that way. But is that all?

Of course, love is a distinguishing mark of the Church (John 13:35). It is the greatest among the gifts (1 Corinthians 13:13). So when people see that a Christian's love goes beyond citizenship, color, and continent; beyond political party or ethnic background, then people want to know more about our Christ and His Church. The church should be the guaranteed place where someone experiences the love of God—and it is! Love is powerful!

Nonetheless, I would look at Scripture where it talks about the kingdom of God, and I noticed how the experience of God's kingdom is vastly different in the Bible than how we experience it in the modern-day church. Jesus said that one evidence of the kingdom would be the expelling of demons (Matthew 12:28). Jesus sent out His disciples to preach, heal, and cast out demons (Luke 10:1-24). The Apostle Paul spoke of God's kingdom saying that it was not just about talk, but power (1 Corinthians 4:20).

It seems like believers in the Bible experienced not only the love of God but supernatural power. People were trained to think, believe, and practice their faith differently than the way we are taught in the 21st century. The first century Church was not concerned about the number of people who showed up, they were more concerned about getting God to show up in power!

Even deacons were different in the Bible. They not only took care of the practical needs of the church and community like they do today (visitation, church maintenance, etc.), but deacons, like Stephen and Philip, would cast out demons, preach, and do individual or mass evangelism. There were more ministerial offices than just the pastor in the Bible. One could be called as an apostle, prophet, evangelist, or teacher. What happened to the intensity, the power, and the diversity of gifts we see in the Bible?

I began to compare the Bible to the modern Church, and I felt so "short-changed." As if we have stopped practicing what the Bible claimed we could be. This is not always the case, but many churches have settled for a business or consumer model of church in which God's people are turned into consumers instead disciples who are meant to advance the kingdom.

After contemplating all of this, I know that there must be people that have felt the way I once did about the Church. You may be a minister, you may belong to a denominational or non-denominational model of church, perhaps you have a scholarly or supernatural approach to the Bible and Christ. Whatever the case may be, you too have resolved in your heart, "There must be more!" Or, you are at least curious.

The reason we have been lacking this power is that many churches are limited to only pastoral leadership. However, when all members of the fivefold are embraced (apostles, prophets, evangelists, pastors, and teachers), then the Church can receive the many gifts of those offices. It's time for the Church to return to its powerful and faith-filled state, where the Church is both scholarly and supernatural!

Are you in the office of pastor, but you struggle in that office—could it be that you belong to a different fivefold office? Are you a Christian that is wondering if you are called to an office or just curious about the topic? Have you ever considered the fivefold to be the governmental structure to guide your church? Do you discount the idea of the fivefold being alive today? However you approach this book, I hope you are at least excited to delve into this subject, and if not, by the end of this book my hope is that you will be.

CHAPTER 1

DEFINING THE FIVEFOLD

As a child, I knew God was calling me to be a minister, but the only terminology I had for becoming a leader in the Church was "pastor." And now, several years later, having moved from childhood to adulthood, and having been involved in multifaceted forms of ministry, I have realized that there is a broad definition for the title "pastor." Therefore, the expectations and functions of a pastor can vary from person to person, association to association, and denomination to denomination. The title "pastor" has become a "catch-all" for ministry, being used for those that are called as an apostle, prophet, evangelist, pastor, or teacher. And this "one size fits all title" has been used for far too long. We have neglected the other offices, and have tried to make everyone fit into this neat package called "pastor," instead of embracing the differences that each calling entails. As a result, I have met people who have questioned their calling to ministry because they did not feel like they were a pastor, and yet, they had sensed a calling to a high level of Christian leadership.

Although the most recognized office in the Christian Church has been limited to the pastor with few exceptions, the Bible seems to imply many offices. There is the office of priest, king, judge, elder, and deacon. And particularly for this book, the offices of the fivefold. So imagine a local church where the highest level of leadership is not just the pastor, but other members of the fivefold. Perhaps one reason a pastor experiences burnout is because they try to carry the burden of all fivefold ministers when there were supposed to be a plurality of other ministers to help with the church's mission. Hence, if someone does not sense they are a pastor, but still believes they are called to church leadership, could it be that they are supposed to exercise that calling as an apostle, teacher, etc.? Are local churches prepared to develop people into offices outside of the pastor?

At this point, you may be asking yourself, "So what exactly is the fivefold ministry? What does it have to do with me? And what does it have to do with the Church?" Perhaps you are reading this book already having a strong comprehension of the fivefold and want to find tangible ways to address and implement it in the local church. Maybe you have little to no knowledge nor experience in this area. You may have noticed that the "catch-all" ministry title of "pastor" does not seem to fit every minister that you have met. If any of the above sounds like you, then you are ready to read this book.

The first concept one needs to understand is that although Jesus left the earth, the christ remains! You may be thinking, "Wait a minute...how can that be?" Because the name "Christ" was not Jesus' last name, but rather, a title representative of who Jesus was and His function on the earth. In the Greek language "Christ" literally means "anointed one." Jesus was the "anointed one" who was empowered to be the Savior of the world. He was anointed to *"proclaim good news to the poor... bind up the brokenhearted, to proclaim freedom for the captives and release from darkness for the prisoners,"* (Isaiah 61:1, NIV). Jesus was the "Christ" because He was anointed by the Holy Spirit, and it was with the Holy Spirit that He did all His good works (Acts 10:38)!

So after Jesus rose from the dead, and before He ascended back to the Father, He promised the apostles that they would receive the gift of the Holy Spirit upon His return to heaven (Acts 1:8-9). In other words, even though Jesus was leaving, the "christ" or the anointing of the Holy Spirit would remain with the apostles—why? So that they could do the work of Christ! Jesus, God in the flesh left, and He will come again, but the christ remains for the believers. We are to pick up the mantle of Christ and do the things that Jesus did while on the earth.

Originally our faith was not called Christianity, it was called "the Way." The first time believers were called "Christians" was in the city called Antioch (Acts 11:25-26). The word "Christian" means "followers of Christ" or "those of Christ." People began to notice the lifestyle of those early believers and in essence said, "Wow, they belong to Christ." They saw the moral, ethical, and powerful witness of believers who knew God; they saw them working with signs, wonders, and miracles like Christ and in essence said, "These believers are 'anointed ones' (christs) of the most high God!"

This is why the Apostle Paul said, *"I have been crucified with Christ and I no longer live, but Christ lives in me,"* (Galatians 2:20a). The Apostle Paul is an "anointed one" of God, he is not claiming to be Jesus Christ, but that Christ does reside in Paul through the anointing of Holy Spirit and thus Paul is Christlike. Dear reader, if you are a believer, then you are Christlike. The world needs to see Christ in you! In one sense, all Christians should be Christlike, people are to look at us and say, "I see Christ in you." But the Apostle Paul goes on to further this description of the christ remaining and having an influence on the earth through a unique group of Christians that are recognized in Ephesians chapter four, and for the sake of this book will be referred to as fivefold ministers (others refer to them as ascension ministers or gifts).

Ephesians Four

Hopefully, we now understand that all Christians are called to be Christlike or "those of Christ." Like Christ, we are anointed to carry on His ministry on the earth. But some believers are called to carry on the mantle of Christ differently from others, specifically through fivefold ministry. Listen carefully to what the Apostle Paul says in Ephesians 4:7-11:

"But to each one of us grace has been given as Christ apportioned it. This is why it says: 'When he ascended on high, he took many captive and gave gifts to his people.' (What does 'he ascended' mean except that he also descended to the lower, earthly regions? He who descended is the very one who ascended higher than all the heavens, in order to fill the whole universe.) So Christ himself gave the apostles, the prophets, the evangelists, the pastors and teachers."

According to the Apostle Paul, Jesus left but the christ remained in the form of the fivefold (I.e., apostles, prophets, evangelists, pastors, and teachers). In the NIV interpretation, the text says that "Christ himself gave," but it could easily be interpreted as "Christ gave of himself." Because Jesus was and is the fivefold ministry. Take some time to look up the following Scriptures and notice how Jesus is the embodiment of all fivefold offices:

Jesus is the Apostle: Hebrews 3:1

Jesus is the Prophet: Mark 6:4

Jesus is the Evangelist: Luke 19:10

Jesus is the Pastor: John 10:11

Jesus is the Teacher: John 1:49

Jesus operated in all these offices in His earthly ministry. Only Jesus was able to hold all the offices simultaneously and I will explain this in greater detail in chapter five. But He calls and commissions others (fivefold ministers) to function in at least one of these offices. Paul goes on to tell us the purpose and the benefits of fivefold ministers:

*"to **equip** his people for works of service, so that the body of Christ may be **built up** until we all reach **unity** in the faith and in the **knowledge** of the Son of God and become **mature**, attaining to the whole measure of the fullness of Christ. Then we will no longer be infants, tossed back and forth by the waves, and blown here and there by every wind of teaching and by the cunning and craftiness of people in their deceitful scheming. Instead, speaking the truth in love, we will grow to become in every respect the mature body of him who is the head, that is, Christ. From him the whole body, joined and held together by every supporting ligament, grows and builds itself up in **love**, as each part does its work."* (Ephesians 4:12-16, emphasis mine)

So here it is. Paul beautifully describes the purpose and benefits of the fivefold:

Equip: I believe there has been a misunderstanding concerning the office of pastor along with the other offices. Some people want to view the fivefold minister as just a friend and if a fivefold minister is just a friend, then everything they say will just be received as a suggestion. When Moses was leading the Israelites, he was not giving suggestions as a friend does, but rather, God was speaking directly to him about what was to be done, and the others were to follow the directions God gave through Moses. When one recognizes the office and function of the fivefold minister, then they understand that they are actually in a position to equip them for their own ministry in the church and the world. God is speaking directly to the fivefold minister concerning how to get everyone involved in ministry.

Nehemiah was the prophet that God called to rebuild the wall in Jerusalem. And while Nehemiah was the one God gave the vision to, Nehemiah had to get others involved to accomplish the mission. Hence, God inspired Nehemiah on precisely how to get the other Israelites involved (Nehemiah 2:17-18, 3). We are not just supposed to associate with fivefold ministers, merely to say we know them, but God has placed these ministers in our lives to help equip us—to train and commission us into the mission field and to be a blessing to other believers.

Build up: When you do not believe in yourself, it's good to have somebody else who does. Peter felt like he lost it all when he denied Christ three times. He had given up on himself and went back to the life he knew before Jesus entered his life. Nevertheless, Jesus still believed in Peter. Over breakfast, Jesus reminded Peter of how important he was to God and the Church (John 21:15-19). Much like Jesus, the fivefold minister will believe in you when you do not believe in yourself. They have been called by God to build you up, even when you feel like all has collapsed.

Unity: When the apostles met in the upper room and the Holy Spirit came upon them, their meeting drew all kinds of people to them. People of different nationalities and languages gathered to see what God was doing. And then, Peter stood before them all and preached a sermon that pointed them to the Lord (Acts 2). In this passage, not only were the apostles in unity as they sought the Lord, but it also caused others to be in unity under the Lordship of Jesus Christ.

Fivefold ministers bring unity to the Body of Jesus Christ. They galvanize people under the banner of Jesus Christ. The Devil thrives in division, and the fivefold minister understands this and seeks to keep the Church unified under the person, work, and principles of Jesus Christ. We are stronger together.

Knowledge: They want to make you knowledgable about God. These ministers are uniquely shaped to teach by word and deed the things of God. We should all be self-feeders, meaning that we know how to pray and search the Scriptures for ourselves. Nonetheless, these ministers will sharpen your understanding in ways you could not have done for yourself.

Nicodemus was deemed as Israel's religious teacher. And yet, he realized in his conversation with Jesus that there were many things he did not understand until engaging with Jesus (John 3:1-21). When an individual is willing to submit themselves to the tutelage of a fivefold minister, their learning grows exponentially.

Mature: As we get older, we begin to look back on our lives and recognize the many ways we were immature in our thinking and actions. We say, "If I knew what I know now, back then, I could have avoided a lot of negative things." The fivefold minister has been placed in your life to help you do that presently. They are significantly mature in the things of the Lord and want to help you mature in your relationship with God and the kingdom.

Samuel had the priest Eli; Elisha had Elijah; and Timothy had Paul. A great spiritual father/mother/mentor wants to see you mature. They believe that they exist for your success and not the other way around. The fivefold minister does not want to make you their fan, they want to make you a mature disciple of the Lord Jesus Christ.

Love: This is the greatest benefit of the fivefold ministry. The greatest commandment is about love (Matthew 22:36-40). The greatest gift is love (1 Corinthians 13:13). Love draws us together with Christ (John 13:35). Love sent our Savior to cross for us (John 3:16). So it makes sense that if a fivefold minister is building us up, giving us knowledge, and maturing us in the name of God, then the fantastic accident of such practice is that we would all grow in love for God, one another, and for the redemption of the world. The fivefold minister is deeply motivated by love because God is love (1 John 4:8).

Before going any further, if I have not made it clear already I will do so now, not everybody is called to be a fivefold minister. Nonetheless, we are all called to represent Christ in one form or another. So if we are not all called to be fivefold ministers, then where do others fall into place? And this is what will be discussed in the next section.

Headship And Body Gifts

Scripture makes it very clear that Jesus is the Head of the Church (Colossians 1:18). He has been crowned Lord of all, He died for the Church, the Church belongs to Christ. But as we have already belabored in the previous section, **Christ distributed His headship responsibilities among the fivefold**. This does not diminish the authority or power of Jesus Christ in any way or make Him less the head of His Church. Jesus simply has entrusted or commanded the fivefold to be good stewards of the headship gifts until He returns. Therefore the fivefold ministers, are subject to Jesus who is the head of the Church, but they carry the responsibility and burdens of governing, guiding, and galvanizing God's people to His commands and principles. To put this in a business analogy, it would be like Jesus is the founder/president, while the fivefold ministers are the vice presidents. They are not the founder/president, but each vice president is authoritative and has responsibilities that represent the desires of the founder/president more so than any manager, assistant, or general employee would.

So the fivefold, while a part of the Body of Christ, uniquely represent the Head, Jesus, in a way the rest of the Body of Christ does not. The head has a heavy responsibility in that it informs the rest of the body. If you hurt your toe or lose a limb, the body can still function. But if you lose your head, the body cannot survive. The head is responsible for governing the rest of the body. Likewise, these fivefold ministers represent the Head of the Church and help govern the Body as Christ leads them.

Does that mean that God loves the fivefold more or deems them as more than the Body? No, of course not! They have a greater responsibility but certainly, the head/fivefold needs to be connected to a body to function. Let's break this down in the following:

Headship/Fivefold Ministers:

* This will be a shorter description of the fuller description that is to come in the future pages.

Apostles: These are the specialized spiritual fathers/mothers, mentors, and pioneers of the faith.

Prophets: They specialize in pointing out the direction of the Lord. They speak the oracles of God personally, locally, and over regions.

Evangelists: These are those that call people to salvation. They are the heralds, they specialize in the proclamation of the gospel and train others to do the same. They bring people into the Church.

Pastors: They specialize in comforting and nurturing the Body of Christ. They are routine examples to a local body of Christlikeness.

Teachers: These specialize in making sure the teaching of the Church is sound. They strengthen the knowledge of Christ and His kingdom for a believer.

Body Ministers:

Elders: God ordains these individuals to support the fivefold minister in their spiritual and pragmatic duties. All fivefold ministers possess the qualifications of what makes for a solid elder. One could say that a fivefold minister is a type of elder that holds a specified, authoritative, and anointed office. But for clarity and distinction in this book, we are going to talk about the fivefold apart from elders. Because not all elders become fivefold ministers but remain a part of the Body. This is what we see happening when Moses needed elders in his ministry:

*"The Lord said to Moses: "Bring me seventy of Israel's elders who are known to you as leaders and officials among the people. Have them come to the tent of meeting, that they may stand there with you. I will come down and speak with you there, and **I will take some of the power of the Spirit that is on you and put it on them**. They will share the burden of the people with you so that you will not have to carry it alone."* (Numbers 11:16-17, emphasis mine)

Notice how God took some of the Spirit that was on Moses and imputed it upon the elders to share the burden with Moses. In other words, Moses' office as a fivefold minister—a prophet—did not diminish just because there were elders appointed to support him. Moses still stood out as the fivefold minister among the elders. These elders were anointed by God to do what? To "stand there with" Moses. The elders did not remove the responsibility Moses had as a fivefold minister but rather they were supposed to support and share the burden. Elders may assist the fivefold minister with praying, preaching, counseling, making spiritual decisions for the church, and the like.

Deacons: God has ordained these individuals to assist the Church in the practical day to day ministries of a local church.

Depending on each church, a deacon may visit the sick, take care of the church grounds and building, be designated administrative duties (collecting offering, etc.), or even within a limited capacity be designated to preach and teach.

Congregation (laity): Every member of the Church is a minister. Not everyone will be in the office of a fivefold, elder, or deacon, but we are all called to minister like Jesus Christ on this earth. The ministers of the congregation will reach people the fivefold minister will never meet. Remember, the fivefold is there to equip the congregation for works of ministry (Ephesians 4:12). So they are sharpening you so that you can sharpen others. Whether a congregation member is at their job, the grocery store, at the park, or on social media, they have the opportunity to minister to others and are gifted to do so.

Fivefold Metaphor

I find it best in retaining the offices and functions of the fivefold by thinking of them as features within a vehicle/car:

Apostles: These would represent the vehicle's frame (chassis). Without the frame, there would not be structure and order for the rest of the car. The frame exists to support the other features on the vehicle. Without the support of the frame, there would be no need for an engine, tires, windshield, or exhaust system. A car would not go anywhere without its frame. Much like the vehicle's frame, the apostle provides structure and order to the Church.

Analogous to how there are dotted and bold lines on streets and highways to keep us in the right lanes and safe, apostles are great at laying out all the boundaries that cause God's Church to flourish. When your arm is out of the socket, you break a bone, or you get a sickness it causes pain in your life. Because whenever structure and order have been compromised things become disjointed and the result is always malfunction and pain. But, the apostle seeks to maintain the integrity of structure and order. The propagation of the Church Universal and the local church has always gone very far because of the pioneering spirit and support of the apostles.

Prophets: You need a GPS or a map to point you in the right direction. The prophet functions like a map or GPS for the Church. They speak or point towards the things that are pleasing to God. The prophet will tell you specifically what is on God's mind concerning you, a nation, a region, and/or the world. Just like your GPS will recalculate your route if you get off on the wrong exit, the prophet is always there to say, "that's not what God wants for you, do this or do that."

Evangelists: The evangelist is the horn of the car. The horn is meant to be loud and draw attention to your car's presence on the road. Once a car horn is blown, everybody looks to see who did it and what is about to happen.

The evangelist draws attention to the gospel story. They have a strong desire to see people accept the gospel of Jesus Christ. They want to bring people into the Church, so wherever they are, they are looking to be a herald of salvation. You need a car horn for safety, without one you might get into a crash that could end your life. The evangelist understands, on a fundamental level, that the greatest crash one could have is an eternity away from the Creator. So they have a unique gift in sharing the gospel in an organized corporate setting or in day to day interactions.

Pastors: Part of what makes the car ride comfortable, is having a heating and cooling system. When it's too hot, just turn on the A/C and let it cool down; when it's too cold, just turn on the heat and let it heat up—either way, the heating and cooling system of your car provides comfort. Likewise, a good pastor knows how to comfort and nurture your faith in a way the other fivefold ministers do not.

Pastors present themselves like good doctors or nurses that have good bedside manner. They truly love being around their congregation and want to see each individual and the families of their congregation produce productive and healthy Christian lives. These are the great counselors of the Body of Christ.

Teachers: Your car needs a certain type of oil, gasoline, or coolant, and a host of other things. The owner's manual informs you on the particular products your car needs. Teachers are the owner's manual for the Church—in that they accurately guide you to the truth. The owner's manual tells you what is appropriate or sound for a certain make and model of vehicle. Likewise, teachers make sure that God's Church has sound teaching that honors the Owner—God.

Vehicles are commonplace in our society. We understand that vehicles move us from place to place. Vehicles represent freedom in that we are not tied down to one location, but we have the means to travel. In essence, the fivefold is the vehicle God has chosen for the Church and when each feature does its part then the Church becomes powerful and progresses towards the vision God has for His Church on earth. Hopefully, this metaphor will help you remember the fivefold simply and adequately. Nonetheless, this is just one metaphor to get you started in conceptualizing fivefold ministry. There is a fuller definition to come in the chapters ahead.

CHAPTER 2

OPPONENTS OF FIVEFOLD MINISTRY

I grew up in the charismatic expressions of Christian faith and without belaboring the circumstances and connections, somehow in God's providence, later on in life, God led me to a traditional and mainline denomination. Today, I see what God did in my life through these two diametrical expressions of Christian faith — God has given me the best of both worlds in that I was engulfed and nurtured in salvation, holiness, righteousness, and the power of the Holy Spirit in my charismatic upbringing; and later, I coupled that sense of fervor with the discipline and understanding of scholarship from a mainline denomination.

What I discovered is that while I have gained so much from both Christian expressions, it seemed neither one of them were able to fully articulate what the fivefold ministry is. In my Charismatic upbringing, some ministers were called apostles or prophets, sometimes both, but there were not many. And of course, there were a plethora of pastors. And while I had a basic understanding of what it meant to be a pastor, the fivefold ministry which also includes apostles, prophets, evangelists, and teachers, was never explained to me personally or taught in the churches that I participated in extensively. Later on, when I joined a traditional mainline denomination, they struggled to define the fivefold ministry for me. Even when I was under the care of this denomination, seeking ordination as a pastor, I remember asking one of my mentors, "Is there room for prophets in this denomination and is there such a thing as modern prophets?" This particular person looked at me somewhat puzzled, said very little about it, and progressed to talk about what makes for a good pastor, skirting around my actual question.

What I'm trying to say is that while some Christian groups have a handle on what the implications and implementations of the fivefold ministry are, the Church as a whole knows very little about the fivefold as prescribed in Ephesians four. The Apostle Paul lays out for us in the New Testament that the Church, under the leadership of Jesus Christ, is governed and directed by apostles, prophets, pastors, evangelists, and teachers. Each role/office is important for the propagation of the Church Jesus built. And while this may be shocking to some, each role/office has its function in the world we live in today, and yet, most Christians and Christian leaders, for that matter, have had few encounters with the fivefold ministry.

For the sake of clarification, the fivefold ministry acknowledges and accepts the function of apostles, prophets, evangelists, pastors, and teachers all operating in the Church and world today. If you only acknowledge and accept the pastor, you do not embrace fivefold ministry. In essence, it's all or nothing. Only embracing one or a few members of the fivefold, does not qualify a local church or ministry to be fivefold. But rather a recognition and acceptance of all fivefold offices are required.

What is interesting, is that there are more instances in the Bible of the title "apostle" or "prophet," than there is "pastor." But it seems the modern Church has pursued the office of a pastor more than the others. Why is this? Well, I believe in part this is because of what I have been alluding to—they are unaware. And because of this, some are intimidated by the notion of the fivefold ministry.

Intimidated By The Fivefold

"It's arrogant to call yourself a prophet." This comment was made by a pastor I respect. We were talking about ministry and as I was sharing my ideas about there being more ministry offices than just the pastor, he did not believe it. I replied to his comment by saying, "How is it any more arrogant to call yourself a 'prophet' than a 'pastor,' since both are mentioned by Paul in Ephesians four and deemed necessary? Why do we only recognize local church leaders as pastors?" My question was met with a puzzled look and a quick change of the subject. What was strange to me, is that the moment I mentioned that somebody could be a real prophet today, this pastor automatically assumed someone with that title must be arrogant. In essence, he was intimidated by his limited experience with people that call themselves prophet and by what he did not understand, so he despised the office of prophet.

Many modern-day Church leaders have accepted and embraced the office of pastor and teacher, and even make an exception for the evangelist in some respects. The pastor is heralded the most at our local churches and many aspiring ministers are trained on how to be a faithful pastor at our Christian institutions of learning. Teachers are acknowledged in our Sunday school classes, small groups, and as professors at seminaries and Bible colleges. And while some find the zeal of the evangelist to be obnoxious, many churches, Christians, and Christian leaders see the necessity of sharing the gospel outside of the church's walls locally and abroad (missions). But, many reject the idea of apostles and prophets or do not know enough about these offices to form a true opinion. However, God intended for the entirety of the fivefold to function in the modern-day church and not just in part. So let me list three reasons people are intimidated:

Cessationists: I was speaking with a deacon of a church, and he told me that his pastor had taught him that apostles do not exist today. It was very clear from that conversation along with other conversations I had with this deacon that he was a cessationist…this being a group of Christians who believe that the gift of prophecy, speaking in tongues, healing, and things of the supernatural perspective have ceased since the apostolic age.

In other words, all of that stuff died along with the apostles mentioned in the Bible.

One of the prominent verses they use to discourage the belief of present-day apostles and prophets, and the supernatural gifts is: *"Love never fails. But where there are prophecies, they will **cease**; where there are tongues, they will be stilled; where there is knowledge, it will pass away,"* (1 Corinthians 13:8, NIV, emphasis mine). Because the Apostle Paul says that one day these gifts will cease, the cessationists believe the gifts are not necessary for today. However, I am fully persuaded that these gifts happen and are necessary for our day and time.

If we were still in the Garden of Eden would we need these offices? Would we need pastors if we were still in the Garden? No, because God would be right there to comfort us. Would we need evangelists? No, because being in the Garden implies that you have already been saved, and since there would be no broken fellowship between you and God, you would not need an evangelist to call you back to God. Would you need a prophet? No, you would speak directly to God in the Garden, and would not need a prophet to tell you the oracles of God. Would you need any of the fivefold ministers, physical healing, or the casting out of demons? Would you need all these seminaries/Bible colleges, shelters, food stations, and the like? The answer is…we would not need any of those things if we were still living in perfect harmony with God in the Garden. But because we are not in the Garden currently, because Jesus has not returned yet, we still live in a fallen world!

Therefore, we still need institutions that teach God's word and provide a haven for Christians to fellowship with other believers. We need Christian humanitarian efforts in a world that is still fallen. And yes, we still need apostles, prophets, evangelists, pastors, and teachers; as these are those God has placed in office over the Church to keep things decent and in order. We still need the casting out of demons, supernatural healings, and the like.

Yes, one-day prophecies will cease as the Apostle Paul articulates, but not until Jesus returns. And although we have the presence of the Holy Spirit in our lives now, who guides us to all truth, and allows us to speak directly to God, the reality is that sometimes we misinterpret what the Spirit is saying to us or we ignore the Holy Spirit altogether. Sometimes life circumstances and/or the troubles we deal with distracts us from the direction of the Holy Spirit. So God will send a prophet to get a person back on track.

In the Old Testament, the Holy Spirit was present to some but not to all as the Spirit is for us New Testament believers. One of those individuals who had the Spirit in the Old Testament was King David (1 Samuel 16:13). Even though he had the Spirit of God in his life to empower him, it was evident that in certain areas of David's life he did not allow the Spirit to guide him, such as in the time of his adultery with Bathsheba. Because David was blinded to his sin, God sent the prophet Nathan to give him a prophetic word concerning his transgression. As we know, David received the prophetic rebuke and then he confessed and repented of his sin (Psalm 51). Likewise, the modern-day Christian, while having the Holy Spirit, can at times be blinded like David, and God will send a prophet to lead a person back to God's will.

Furthermore, when Paul talks about the fivefold ministry in Ephesians four, he does mention a marker or indicator for when the fivefold will come to an end. Essentially he states, the fivefold will continue to be necessary, *"until we all reach unity in the faith and in the knowledge of the Son of God and become mature, attaining to the whole measure of the fullness of Christ,"* (13). When the Church is split over doctrines, race, and/or denominational lines does it seem like we have unity as the Scripture indicates? Has the entire Body of Christ reached maturity in the faith? Have we attained the whole measure of the fullness of Christ? The obvious answer is no! And it seems like we will be working towards this until Christ comes.

Therefore, the fivefold and every office it entails is a necessary ministry in pursuit of this ideal.

God is so graceful to give the Church—both of the past and the modern era—apostles, prophets, evangelists, pastors, and teachers. God—in His grace—still performs miracles, allows us to speak in heavenly tongues, prophesy, and cast out demons. If one is not convinced already, hopefully, by the end of this book, they will accept the fullness of God's gifts to the Church and the world.

AntiChrist Spirit: The Apostle John once said, *"Dear children, this is the last hour; and as you have heard that the antichrist is coming, even now many antichrists have come,"* (1 John 2:18). John was telling the Church that many false christs are coming into the world and that while some of their acts may appear to be christlike, they are not from God. Jesus even said that people will begin to appear claiming to be the Messiah although they are not (Matthew 24:5). The antichrist spirit is the counterfeit of the real Christ, seeking to resemble the truth, yet deceiving many people.

A great example of the antichrist spirit is demonstrated in Acts 16:16-18. There was a fortune-teller who would predict the future by the help of a demonic spirit. When godly men such as Paul and Silas passed her by, she began to follow them while yelling that they were men of God who preached the gospel. Eventually, Paul became annoyed by her presence and he casts the spirit/demon out of her. What is of note is that the woman was telling the truth while under the influence of a demon—they were men from God and they did preach the gospel as she exclaimed. One could even conclude that she was "prophesying" like a prophet. Herein lies the craftiness of the Devil in that he will deceive by using the truth!

It is no different from what the Devil did in the Garden of Eden. He told the first generation of human beings that if they ate the fruit of the tree of knowledge of good and evil, they would have insight concerning good and evil. And that was exactly what God had told them, however, the Devil used that truth to entice them away from God—it was a deceptive or distorted version of the truth. It's empirically important to understand that there are people in the world today that are full of the antichrist spirit. They may preach, prophesy, heal, do benevolent acts, and display many powers under the influence of demons. This is evident in Matthew 7:21-23, where it says:

"Not everyone who says to me, 'Lord, Lord,' will enter the kingdom of heaven, but only the one who does the will of my Father who is in heaven. Many will say to me on that day, 'Lord, Lord, did we not prophesy in your name and in your name drive out demons and in your name perform many miracles?' Then I will tell them plainly, 'I never knew you. Away from me, you evildoers!'"

Jesus makes it very clear that some people can perform various signs and wonders, and yet, they were never in a relationship with Jesus. The Apostle Paul informs us that Satan pretends to be an angel sent by God (2 Corinthians 11:14). The antichrist spirit will imitate godly activity in an attempt to draw people away from God. Nevertheless, all preaching, teaching, prophecy, signs and wonders, etc., when they are from God, will cause us to grow in a greater admiration for Jesus and produce the fruit of the Holy Spirit (Galatians 5:22-26). The Christian is not authenticated by signs and wonders, but by the fruit, they produce as Jesus stated in Scripture (Matthew 7:16).

Because Christians struggle to differentiate between the real and the fake; because Christians struggle to discern what is of God and not of God, some elect to disregard any notion of modern-day apostles and prophets (other fivefold ministers outside of the pastor, teacher, and evangelist), and the supernatural workings of the Spirit. Jesus said that we, His Church, would do greater works than Himself (John 14:12).

Certainly, Jesus was including all fivefold ministers concerning the Church doing greater things.

In-fighting: Because there are many individuals and governing denominational/associational bodies that do not comprehend the fivefold ministry, there is in-fighting instead of support. What I mean is that one minister criticizes another saying, "How come that minister doesn't do a gospel presentation at the end of every service and teach the congregation to do the same?" It could be that the minister is a true pastor who cares for the flock. So the minister who is in the office of the pastor will talk about salvation and the gospel—it is serious to the pastor. But the God-given disposition and function of the pastor is to care for the flock holistically. So, they may spend more time talking about family life, marriage, caring for the sick, and the like.

However, if you have a person with the title of "pastor" but they actually hold the office of evangelist, then they will be more likely to give a gospel presentation at the end of each service, and do sermon series and classes on how to be a greater witness for Christ. And so it is…when ministers do not have a proper understanding of each office, they devalue and reject one another. One says,"That preacher should be more prophetic," the other says, "That preacher should be more apostolic," and another says, "That preacher should teach more." And the cycle continues.

Some have built entire denominations and associations on one office. Hence, a true evangelist enrolls into a seminary, but this particular seminary only instructs from the office of pastor or teacher. Likewise, the prophet has a lot of dreams and visions from God, but unfortunately, they attend a ministry school/ college that does not believe true prophets exist anymore. And they are told that if you hear the Lord speaking to you, do not tell anyone, because they might think you have lost your mind. This is not to say that there cannot be individual schools that focus on one discipline, so long as they maintain an appreciation for other offices.

But I assert that more often than not, the reason many Christian institutions focus on one, maybe two offices is because they just have not been taught about the fivefold ministry. Therefore, we get this nasty in-fighting. Because ministers are trained with only one ministerial focus. And it's time that ministers begin to have an understanding and appreciation for all fivefold ministers and not just the ones they are comfortable with.

Due to cessationists beliefs, the influence of the antichrist spirit, and the in-fighting among ministers, many have struggled to accept the fivefold ministry; others believe in the fivefold, but have had limited knowledge concerning this subject, and therefore criticize other fivefold ministers. Whatever category one may fall into I am asking you, the reader, to suspend whatever it is you know or do not know, believe or disbelieve for the duration of this book, so that you may get a fresh biblical view of why fivefold ministry is so important.

The fivefold ministry, while subversive to many, has always been operating in the Church of Jesus Christ. What this book has to offer is not a new revelation—perhaps for some, it will be —but rather, a tangible definition of what is already in the Bible. What was plain to those early Christians, should be plain and celebrated among us today. If for any reason, you have any doubts concerning fivefold ministry…then I ask you to pray the exact request one man made to Jesus concerning the supernatural: *"'I do believe; help me overcome my unbelief,'"* (Mark 9:24b). I believe you are reading this book because you want to understand more, you want to believe. Having now acknowledged some of the ignorance or apprehension toward the fivefold ministry, let us now define it in chapter three with open minds and a spirit of grace.

CHAPTER 3

WHICH OFFICE IS THE BEST

One of the questions you might be asking is, "Who is the best among the fivefold?" Some of you might think it's the pastor (shepherd) because even Jesus spoke of Himself as a shepherd (John 10:11). You might think it's the teacher because as Jesus traveled people referred to Him as a teacher (Mark 14:45). You may say it's the prophet because Jesus spoke of Himself in the third person as a prophet (Matthew 13:57). However, no single fivefold member is better than the other. Was Jesus more important on earth when He was operating as an apostle than when He was operating as a pastor? Of course not! All five offices were parts of the whole measure of who Jesus was while on earth. All offices are valued and needed. They all administer, govern, and guide; it's just that each fivefold office comes with a different responsibility and anointing.

Order Of Importance?

Some attempt to make the apostle or the prophet the most important of the fivefold. And I believe to do so reveals a common flaw of humanity, whereby we constantly compare and contrast ourselves to others in an attempt to be superior. Two disciples (James and John) succumbed to this small thinking when debating about who would sit on the right or left side next to Jesus' throne when His kingdom arrived. But Jesus redirected the entire conversation and He began to talk about service as being the more noble pursuit instead of lording over other people (Mark 10:35-45). The same is true with the conversation of the fivefold ministry. People want to know which office is the best, the most powerful, or the most important.

However, there is no definitive Scripture concerning a hierarchy of importance within the fivefold. If one wants to make the argument perhaps the closest verse to such a claim is what we find in 1 Corinthians 12:28: *"And God has placed in the church first of all apostles, second prophets, third teachers, then miracles, then gifts of healing, of helping, of guidance, and of different kinds of tongues."* So if this is about the order of importance, then what about the pastors and the evangelists... where do they fall in the rank?—Paul does not even bother to mention them in this Scripture—are they not important?

Perhaps if we take what Paul says in this Scripture and connect it with Ephesians four, then we will see the order of importance? In Ephesians 4:11 the order in which Paul names each office is as follows: "So Christ himself gave the apostles **(1)**, the prophets **(2)**, the evangelists **(3)**, the pastors **(4)** and teachers **(5)**," (emphasis mine). If we were to interpret or impose that Paul must have listed each office in order of importance, then he would be contradicting himself here. Because in Ephesians four the third most important is the evangelist, but in the Corinthian verse the third most important is the teacher and the evangelist is left out! So which is it? The answer is that it's inconclusive. Or to be more precise, there is no hierarchy of importance among the fivefold.

* It is undeniable that the apostle and prophet have been given a greater or weightier responsibility than the other fivefold offices. A foundation has to be strong to support a building. And being that they represent the foundation of the Church (Ephesians 2:20), they have carried a heavier burden. Their uniqueness is even represented in that apostles and prophets are responsible for writing the majority of the Bible. The difference between apostles/prophets and the other offices is the greater responsibility or burden they carry, but they are not of greater value or importance than any other office. A foundation (apostle and prophet) would be pointless if there was nothing to build on

top of it such as the walls, roof, etc. *(evangelist, pastor, and teacher)*. All of these are equally essential when constructing a building.

Order Of Operation

While there is not a single verse or a collection of verses one can put together to claim a hierarchy of importance without contradiction, I do believe there is an order of operation, particularly in how God established the Church. The Bible teaches that the Church is "...built on the foundation of the apostles and prophets," (Ephesians 2:20a). So there is a "foundation" or starting point—an order of operation. This meaning that all fivefold ministers are necessary, important, and one cannot do without the other—one impacts another.

Think of the order of operations when solving a math problem. We can look at an equation as simple as "50-20x2" to see the importance of following the order of operations. You see, if you simply try to solve this equation in the order it is written your thinking would look like this: 50-20=30; 30x2=60; therefore your final answer would be 60. And you would be incorrect. Instead you need to follow the correct order of operations, or PEDMAS for short (parenthesis, exponents, division and multiplication, addition and subtraction), in order to solve the equation properly. By following PEDMAS your solution would look like this: 20x2=40; 50-40=10. So your answer would be 10. And this would be correct. What a difference following the correct order of operations makes in solving such a simple problem!

To solve the problem, we had to follow a sequence of operations. If we skip over the succession of the order we will not solve the mathematical equation, or at least not correctly. And if we really have no idea, the best we can do is give an educated guess.

Nobody in their right mind would say, a certain step in the above equation is unimportant or unnecessary. No, each step has a certain function that helps solve the problem. Each step is authoritative in its own right and has a significant impact on the final result. You cannot solve the problem without going through each step in its proper order. Likewise, there is an order of operation within the fivefold. And—I believe—by understanding the biblical definition of each office, one can see the New Testament fivefold order of operations of how God establishes a church. Allow me to suggest the order in the following...

Apostle (step one): The Apostle Paul started many New Testament churches and activated and trained ministers like Timothy. Hence, God sends (apostle means "sent") the apostle to break ground in new territories; to establish new churches, ministers, and provide structure and order for the new endeavor God is doing. Moreover, apostles are responsible for receiving new revelation from the Lord that becomes a doctrine in which the Church adheres to. Paul's revelation of salvation alone in the book of Romans is what many modern-day Christians use to explain the mystery of the gospel.

Prophet (step two): After the ground has been broken by an apostle, then the question becomes, "What is God saying to a particular church/community?" What is the direction for a said community of faith? The Prophet Jeremiah gave a specific word to the Israelites in exile. They were already an established community of faith, but they needed a directive from God. In essence, Jeremiah tells the people to continue to be productive while in captivity (Jeremiah 29). The prophet points people to greater admiration of God (Isaiah 6), the prophet reminds the Church to be holy and to continue their faithfulness to God (Isaiah 58:1).

Evangelist (step three): The new church has been established by an apostle, the prophet gives a clear proclamation of what God wants for said community, and now the church needs to be filled with people. The evangelist goes out as a herald of the gospel and tells the beautiful story of redemption to whoever will listen and invites them to become a part of the Church. Philip was an evangelist and when he would share the gospel, people would be converted, baptized, and became a part of the Church (Acts 8).

Pastor (step four): The apostle has started a new church, the prophet proclaims God's direction for a said body of believers, the evangelist brings in new converts, and now the pastor comforts and nurtures the congregation's faith; through practical, relational, and comforting application. Jesus was relational by enjoying regular meals and attending celebrations with His disciples (John 2:1-12). James, who pastored the church in Jerusalem, gave practical counsel on how to live and treat people in a God-honoring way. The pastor reminds the congregation of the importance and encouragement of regular fellowship with believers.

Teacher (step five): Now having gone through the functions of the apostle, prophet, evangelist, and pastor; it's time for the one that reinforces what has been taught and/or experienced. The teacher enhances the church's knowledge on the tenets of the faith. They are great at giving a further explanation to the revelation you received from an apostle, the oracle from a prophet, the gospel story you heard from an evangelist, and the counsel you received from a pastor. The teacher goes about maintaining and furthering the discussion of what has been established. They make sure the congregation's learning remains sound, accurate, and faithful—this is what Luke sets out to do with his Gospel (Luke 1:1-4).

Just like a math problem, when this fivefold order of operation happens, problems get solved. We can have a major impact on the world when all offices are functioning. We can no longer limit the Church to the "catch-all" pastor. We need all the offices operating for the glory of God. Therefore, one should not conclude that one office is better than the other. Nonetheless, while I assume one could renegotiate this order of operation, this does seem to be the typical New Testament cycle in which God propagates His Church in the world.

Can Operate With Other Gifts

While there is a distinction to each office, a fivefold minister in some capacity, can operate with the other giftings outside of their office. It's a requirement for the apostle to be good at operating in the gifts of other offices. However, there may be occasions where God has someone in the office of a teacher, pastoring a church; or a prophet teaching a class on Church doctrine like one does in the office of teacher. The Spirit of God is not limited to an office. All fivefold ministers can establish structure and order like the apostle, operate in the prophetic like the prophet, share the gospel like the evangelist, bring comfort to the Body like the pastor, and teach foundational truths like the teacher if this is what God allows them to do for a time. A father may not be as nurturing as a mother can be in the typical sense, nonetheless, there are moments where a father may come across as nurturing to a child when necessary. Likewise, there are moments where an evangelist, might come across as an apostle and vice versa.

Just imagine a high school where there is a gym teacher who wanted to learn Spanish because his class would be receiving a foreign student from Columbia in the next trimester. This teacher was informed that the student was "okay" at English but was most confident when speaking in Spanish. One the day the gym teacher visits the Spanish teacher whose office was down the hall from his office. He asks the Spanish teacher to give him some basic words to greet the new student in her native tongue. When the new student arrives at his class, he excitedly greets her by saying, "Hola y bienvenidos a nuestra clasé." And the new student immediately started speaking back to him in full paragraphs of Spanish. The teacher looking puzzled at her speech, he finally says, "I'm so sorry, I only know that one phrase in Spanish."

For a brief moment, it seemed like this gym teacher was like the Spanish teacher. However, the new student quickly found out that he did not have the level of proficiency like a Spanish teacher to hold a conversation. Could the gym teacher pick up more phrases over time to communicate with the new student? Absolutely! But he is much better at being a gym teacher, than a Spanish instructor because that is the office he is trained and equipped for—the gym teacher is limited in Spanish. Therefore, if this student wants to have a great conversation with a teacher in her native language, it would be wise for her to pay a visit to the Spanish teacher.

This scenario relates to the fivefold because each office functions with the same Spirit. Hence, a prophet may be able to periodically operate in the teaching gift like the teacher. Likewise, a teacher may be able to operate in the prophetic, as the Spirit leads them, like the prophet. Nonetheless, the prophet and the teacher hold different offices that come with different responsibilities, anointing, functions, and disposition as do all the others.

Whenever you are in a fivefold office, you always have access to the gifts or functions of your office. For example, if you are a prophet, you easily have access to the prophetic functions (word of knowledge, word of wisdom, prophecy, dreams, etc.) The only moment a prophet cannot operate prophetically is due to disobedience or because God is not speaking through the prophet at the time. Nonetheless, the prophet can operate prophetically automatically, whereas operating pastorally is not as automatic. They can operate pastorally, but in a limited capacity because it's not the office they hold. However, if a person holds more than one office, they may have full capacity of those offices. In chapter five we will discuss having multiple offices in greater detail in a section entitled, "More Than One Office?"

CHAPTER 4

WHICH OFFICE IS THE BEST PART TWO

While in the last chapter we talked about how all fivefold offices are needed and one is not better than the other, still people tend to believe the apostle is the best of the fivefold. Because God requires the apostle to pioneer new ministries, establish the kingdom of God in new territories, and equip new ministers; the apostle must have at least a basic, practical, and practiced understanding of all the spiritual gifts, whereas the other fivefold are not required to. The apostle is like the "jack of all trades," yet, not necessarily having the same level of proficiency as those who hold the other offices for said gifts. Nonetheless, the office of an apostle is great at activating, training, and establishing new fivefold leaders. So even though the apostle may be "good" at sharing the gospel and the evangelist is "great" at it, the apostle is still gifted to provide structure, order, correction, and training to help the evangelist and the Church's evangelistic efforts advance from "great" to "greater." The apostle is like a coach who knows the right information and training methods to make someone better at their craft.

Furthermore, some people believe the apostle holds all five offices. And this is not true. The apostle can operate with all the spiritual gifts of each office, but that does not mean they hold every office. The apostle is like a Swiss Army knife or multi-tool. This instrument has various tools for different occasions all housed in one. They usually have a bottle opener, screwdriver, knife, saw, and pliers among other features. These features are meant to be decent or at least good, but they are not meant to replace the much stronger, bigger, more efficient, and single version of each tool found on the multi-tooled device. In other words, the small saw on your multi-tool, will not be able to cut down an entire tree as a standard saw or chain saw. The small knife will not be able to cut through meat like a cleaver or butchers knife. Likewise, the apostle can operate prophetically, but not like someone who is in the office of prophet.

As mentioned, an apostle is a pioneer. As such, they tend to be the first in establishing a new work of God. Therefore, the apostle must be able to relate to all of the offices to some degree, to help sharpen and train others of a new revelation—to help others to be great at the gifts of their office. So naturally, because of the apostle's gift set, they tend to be the visionary leader of a local congregation and have other ministers, churches, and different types of ministries under their oversight. Nonetheless, this does not make the apostle the greatest among the fivefold nor does it mean that because an apostle is present at a church that they automatically become the visionary leader.

Visionary Leader

The visionary leader can be any fivefold minister to whom the Lord has entrusted the vision and the mission of a local church. Traditionally, we always assume the pastor to be the visionary leader. But what if the person God has entrusted the vision/mission to is the evangelist of a local church body. Yes, there may be an apostle, prophet, pastor, and teacher present at a local church to equip and strengthen the congregation, but should the evangelist have some apostolic gifting, even though they do not hold the office of an apostle, the evangelist could be the visionary leader!

What I am trying to say is that maturity and God's sovereign choice is a factor (Matthew 22:14). Should there be a newly ordained apostle and a seasoned pastor present in the same congregation, but the pastor has already matured to great heights in their office and relationship with God. Then, God might entrust the vision of a local church to a pastor over the apostle at the church who is at the beginning stages of growth in their office. Remember, Esau was the firstborn son that was entitled to an inheritance, however, the inheritance went on to Jacob because he matured enough to handle it (Genesis 25:19-34). Likewise, ideally an apostle makes for a great visionary leader, but God may chose the seasoned pastor, teacher, etc., to be the visionary leader of a local congregation. So, if a pastor is the visionary leader of a local congregation, where there is also an apostle present, and that apostle was not responsible for training up the pastor and establishing the church, then that apostle does not override the pastor who is the visionary leader God has put in place. The reason God has chosen to reveal certain things to the visionary leader and not to the other fivefold who are present at a local congregation is that God knows the visionary leader can handle the responsibility and delegation of the vision and mission. Therefore, an apostle would still function in all their apostolic functions, while maintaining respect to the authority of the visionary leader God has put in place over the local congregation. The apostle could still train other leaders at the church, seek out new territory to establish new churches, and aid the visionary leader. Again, all of the fivefold members are valuable, but for there to be order and not chaos, God will choose one out of the fivefold to delegate the vision and mission God has for a local congregation.

For greater clarification, imagine a world-renowned chef comes to visit you at your home. This chef is rated as the greatest chef in the world and has decided to help you make a new dish in your home. But just because this world-class and famous chef is in your kitchen, does not mean they replace you as the main cook of your house! Why is that...because it's your kitchen. While the renowned chef has great techniques and skills to aid your cooking, this chef would not know where all your utensils are, what items you have in the pantry or refrigerator, and does not know exactly what everybody likes to eat in your house. You would still be the main or visionary cook of your house. The chef would just be there to make you better and help feed the other people of the house. Are you getting the analogy? The same is true of a church house. The visionary leader could be any member of the fivefold. But some find this hard to believe because for so long, we have only embraced the office of pastor as the visionary leader and perhaps in other church expressions, the apostle. So let us continue the thought of the visionary leader being an evangelist. And this particular evangelist runs and leads the major organizational meetings of the church, and does the preaching. Remember just because this person is in the office of an evangelist, does not mean this person cannot operate in pastoral gifting, it just means they do not necessarily have the level of accessibility and proficiency as those that hold said office. Therefore, if God has placed an evangelist as the visionary leader of a church house, it could be because the individual mission of that church is to be extremely and uniquely evangelistic in the community the church is located in. So while the evangelist is the main driver of the vision and mission of this imagined church, ideally God will raise other fivefold leaders or members of the body to help the evangelistic visionary leader and the congregation, in its apostolic, prophetic, pastoral, and teaching endeavors. Every visionary leader God chooses is unique but not every visionary leader is a grandfather leader, and we will delve into that topic in the next section.

Grandfather Leader

I mentioned in the previous section how apostles may have other fivefold members under their oversight. But can apostles apostle other apostles (I know the wording sounds strained in this sentence)? In essence, can one apostle sharpen another apostle? The answer is, yes!

In many Christian circles, there is what is called the "chief apostle" or "apostle of apostles" or "bishop." I personally like the term or analogy of "grandfather" to describe this type of leadership. While there are spiritual mothers and fathers, for sake of simplicity, let's use the example of a father and son to speak to the whole. Simply put, a grandfather is a father of a father or fathers. The grandfather, who has matured through the process of fathering his own son(s) now has the privilege and knowledge of helping his son(s), in their fathering efforts (Proverbs 13:22).

This is just to say that there are those apostles that have matured and have been graced to the place of being able to influence others of the same office. One may be an apostle (father) who has several ministries under their oversight, but the grandfather apostle has other apostles under their oversight along with other ministries.

The typical consensus among churches is that Peter was a grandfather apostle in that he received revelation many other apostles did not, and he distributed this revelation to the other apostles to teach and practice—hence, showing himself to be a grandfather apostle among the others (Acts 10, 15:1-21). Moreover, Paul was called to the Gentiles (Acts 9:15) and was also one of the few apostles who had this revelation before many of the others did. Peter and Paul's revelation was propagated by the others. In essence, Peter and Paul apostled other apostles—they stood out from among them. From Peter's shadow healing people (Acts 5:15) to people getting healed by touching Paul's handkerchiefs (Acts 19:12), all are evidence of how they were frontrunners in apostolic leadership.

Generally speaking, a grandfather leader is often a person in the office of apostle but this is not always the case. Remember, every fivefold minister has distinctives related to said office, nonetheless, one office may also have limited graces of another office (E.g., a pastor may be able to prophesy even though they are not a prophet). Therefore, if a fivefold minister, outside of the apostle, has been graced with an ability to lead leaders, like the apostle, then they too, can be a grandfather leader. There can be a pastor of pastors, evangelist of evangelists, and so on. The Prophet Samuel was graced to be a leader of other prophets. He had a school of prophets that he trained (1 Samuel 19:20). Nicodemus was also recognized as a teacher among teachers (John 3:10).

It's important to reiterate that we should not think of the fivefold ministers in terms of who is the best, they each have different responsibilities and giftings. Each office has a disposition and function that serves the Body of Christ and the world. And each office mutually benefits the others. But beyond the mutuality among the five offices, there could be one particular office member that ranks up to the place of grandfather leader—becoming the leader of leaders. We even see that among the twelve disciples, it was Peter, James, and John that seemed to be the grandfathers among the other disciples (Luke 8:51, Matthew 17:1-2, Matthew 26:36-39). It was not that Jesus loved the other disciples less, it's just that Peter, James, and John, were called to a greater degree of responsibility.

The grandfather leader is nuanced from the visionary leader. Meaning that every grandfather leader must be a visionary but not every visionary leader is a grandfather leader. In other words, the visionary leader is equipped to carry the vision for a particular context or mission. However, the grandfather leader stands out among those of the same office and can build organizations, schools, and chart a vision for an entire network. These are often the leaders of an entire denomination, associations, or movements (E.g., Martin Luther, John Wesley, Phoebe Palmer, etc.). And you will notice that depending on what office the grandfather leader holds, that office becomes the emphasis of said denomination, association, or movement. If the grandfather leader is a teacher, then scholarship is usually emphasized. If the grandfather leader is a prophet, then the prophetic is usually emphasized.

An Office Cannot Be Judged By Preaching

Why is it always the pastor who is the main preacher of our local congregations? While this is not true of every pastor, sometimes, you may have a pastor who is good at pastoring the flock in terms of counseling, mentoring, and prayer; but they are inadequate as a preacher. And it's unfortunate that in the modern era we judge how called, anointed, gifted, or talented a minister is, based on how they preach. In my book, *Shattered Pulpits,* I talk about how the pastor does so much more than just preaching:

> *"People often fail to realize the amount of work a true pastor puts in. I have known pastors that have talked people out of suicide, helped brings families back together, answered phone calls of hurting people in the middle of the night, and the like. It is no stretch of the imagination to say that pastors save peoples' lives. They also deal with the pressure of realizing that one day they will stand before God for every sermon, counseling session, how they managed church funds, and the list goes on and on. A pastor never clocks out. They know that who they are privately as well as publicly will have an impact on their congregation and the community they serve...Pastors do the work of counselors; they are spiritual surgeons; they are as good as, if not better than professional/motivational speakers; they save lives like a firefighter; some have great social and networking skills that are parallel to the greatest of entrepreneurs; they are life coaches who come beside you and help you in areas of leadership and more. Oftentimes they are just as available to the congregation as you would expect a 911 dispatcher to be; some have attained master's degrees in theology and*

pastoral care; others have great administrative and managerial skills. And yet, while they do the job of a professional counselor, a 911 dispatcher, a life coach, speaker, etc., and some having even attained degrees to benefit the people they serve, there are still those that assume a pastor should not be supported financially. In short, I personally have had pastors make sacrifices for me to be successful (you pastors in my life know who you are). There are pastors that have spent hours in prayer for me. Therefore, I believe a true pastor never gets paid enough. Some pastors will elect to work another job on top of their already pressured calling of being a pastor." (18-19)

Preaching, is without a doubt, a major part of what the pastor does, however, the pastor is required to know and participate in a lot of things. Nevertheless, there are cases when a pastor does not possess the fluidity of speech like great orators…so does that mean they are inadequate pastors? No, of course not, while they may not be the best public speakers, they still faithfully convey God's will, possibly through means other than preaching. Typically speaking, the offices that usually have the stronger preaching graces are the apostle, prophet, and evangelist. Nonetheless, churches could have a called, anointed, and highly skilled pastor in their midst, but if their pastor is an "okay" preacher, they judge their pastor as not being very anointed or gifted. It's because the modern Church, for far too long, has not had a proper understanding of the disposition and function of each office and how they fulfill God's plan for the Body of Christ.

Have you ever considered that a good pastor may not have to be the main preacher of a church house? Have you ever considered that if a pastor does not have a strong preaching grace, then maybe that pastor should not handle the bulk of the preaching for the calendar year? That pastor should preach, but not every Sunday. Maybe the ordained evangelist or prophet could handle the bulk of preaching? Or if there are no other fivefold offices present at the church, how about this: a pastor, who is the visionary leader of a church house, recognizes they do not have great preaching graces, so the pastor allows a deacon, elder, or a congregation member who has preaching graces to participate in the regular peaching endeavor? This is all to say that the fivefold is more than preaching. As you go further in the book, hopefully, you will come to understand this, if you have not already.

Accepting The Fivefold

I have met many Christian organizations, churches, and individual believers who have embraced the fivefold and as a result, their ministries are flourishing in ways God intended. However, at large, the Church has very little understanding and/or experience with the fivefold ministry. As a result, churches are not as vibrant and strong as they could be. The Church was meant to operate with more than just the pastor. But the pastor seems to be the main if not, the only office Christian organizations embrace without hesitation. Hence, some pastors are struggling to be pastors, because that is not the office they hold but it's the only office that is recognized and available! Or it's the only office that people know how to train them for.

Suppose a person in the office of the prophet becomes a pastor of a local church. Now, unless the Lord has given this prophet some pastoral graces (or holds more than one office which we will discuss later), this prophet is going to struggle in the office of pastor. Why? Because when you look at biblical prophets did they spend a lot of time at parties and visiting people for fellowship and pastoral care or counseling? No, oftentimes prophets were lonely. They spent their time primarily around God. Biblical prophets were not the life of the party but were told to refrain from casual parties. Just look at what God demanded of the Prophet Jeremiah: "*...do not enter a house* *where there is feasting and sit down to eat and drink,"* (Jeremiah 16:8). Jeremiah, along with other prophets, often spent more time with God than people. Biblically speaking, they often showed up around people, when it was time to release the oracles of God.

The congregation whose "pastor" is a prophet will notice that their "pastor" is a great preacher, because prophets often are. But they will also notice that their "pastor" does not have a desire for home visits nor are they the best at being sympathetic or empathic during one on one counseling sessions because that is what a true pastor is great at! What I'm trying to say is that there are "pastors" who are really prophets, and they feel more comfortable preaching, praying, and prophesying, than going to graduation parties, barbecues, and having long casual conversations over the phone—they may truly want to be alone with God, not because they do not love people, but rather, biblically speaking, God always nurtures and strengthens His prophets in loneliest. The prophets would spend time in desert places and caves with God. If the congregation does not realize their "pastor" is a prophet, then they might think their "pastor" is not a good one.

So it is that you have "pastors" who are struggling because God has called them into a different fivefold office, but they are told that they have to be pastors. And you have churches that are struggling to mobilize and be what God has called them to be, because if all the church wants is comforting and nurturing that comes from a pastor, they may never experience what the other fivefold ministers could help the Church to become (I.e., apostolic, prophetic, evangelistic, and scholarly). In essence, I have seen churches that were prophetic because their visionary leader was a prophet, but they were not scholarly because they did not have a person in the office of teacher present. I have seen highly evangelistic churches because their visionary leader was an evangelist, but they did not have much structure and order to their church because someone in the office of apostle was not present.

For the Church to be healthy and reach maturity, we need to embrace the fivefold ministry as God intended. The fivefold is what God instituted per the Scripture (Ephesians 4). It's not a charismatic idea, it's not something that only took place in biblical times, but it's for our time. And it's about time, we start doing church God's way.

CHAPTER 5

BECOMING A FIVEFOLD MINISTER

Being a happily married man and a father of four children, there are times when my wife and I need to get a babysitter so that we can have a date night. We always make sure to give the babysitter detailed instruction on how to care for our children while we are away. We inform the sitter on what medications our children need, emergency phone numbers, the general house rules; and sometimes, we have even left the sitter a spare house key in case of an emergency in which our children need to be taken out of the house.

In essence, the babysitter represents my wife and me by proxy. The sitter has been given some authority to represent the wishes and standards we have set as parents, but the sitter does not, by any stretch of the imagination, have full authority as my wife and I do. Furthermore, the sitter has limited or prescribed authority given to them which only lasts for the duration of babysitting our children. So within reason, the sitter has limited access to spaces in my house and I expect the sitter to hold my children accountable and keep the house in order until my wife and I return. However, if I returned home, only to discover that the sitter invited unauthorized guests into my house, took a nap in my bedroom, and even spanked some of my children—that would be crossing the line. Because while the sitter has been given limited authority to act on behalf of the parents, the sitter is not the parents and does not have the right to physically discipline my children, have access to spaces such as my bedroom, and invite people over that I did not allow. The sitter is only acting on behalf of the parents but indeed does not have the office of the parent. In the same manner, you may have certain gifts resembling that of a fivefold minister, but that does not mean you hold an office.

King Saul was not a prophet. Nonetheless, when Saul was in the company of other prophets he was able to prophesy (1 Samuel 10:10). In other words, King Saul was only able to prophesy when he was around other prophets! Someone in the office of prophet carries the prophetic anointing with them everywhere they go. A prophet can always operate prophetically. Now immediately, one might say, "How can that be?" And yet, people with the gift of tongues can speak in tongues as often as they want to! The Apostle Paul talked about how he wished all would speak in tongues (1 Corinthians 14:5) and he even claimed to have spent more time speaking in tongues than all of those at the Corinthian church (1 Corinthians 14:18). Faith is another gift of the Spirit that we all have access to and can operate in whenever we want (1 Corinthians 12:9). And since the only way I can be pleasing to God is by living and operating in faith (Hebrews 11:6), then I should be pursuing faith joyfully as often as I can.

Full Access

It's important to understand that when one is in an office they have full access to the functions of said office. When one is in the office of prophet, they have access to all the prophetic gifts and can implement them at will, so long as God wants to speak a word to an individual, group, or region. In other words, as a prophet, I know that I can give anybody a word from God. As a prophet, God has entrusted and granted me access to all the prophetic functions. The only time I cannot give someone a prophetic word is not because I do not have access to the giftings, but because God does not want to speak a word to a person(s) at that moment. I have had this happen before in a meeting, where I gave prophetic words to everyone except one person. And when she asked me why I said nothing to her, I said, "Because the Lord hasn't given me something to say to you."

A prophet does not have limited access to the prophetic gifts, however, God may limit the prophet on how much to say or tell them not to say anything all. But someone who belongs to the Body does have limited access to the prophetic gifts. Like King Saul, one may only be able to prophesy when around other prophets or for specific situations. There may be an elder, deacon, or congregation member who can operate strongly in one area of the prophetic gifts such as the "word of knowledge," in which God reveals to them a revelation concerning an individual's past or present situation. And God may use this individual a lot in the "word of knowledge," but they do not carry the same responsibility or disposition of the prophet. Remember, the babysitter does not have the same authority as the parent. Just because one has gifts related to an office, does not mean they hold an office.

Title Represents A Disposition

Disposition and personality are not the same thing. Disposition is about the arrangement, placement, or framework of how someone or something is inclined to perform under a given circumstance. Whereas personality is comprised of qualities relating to each person and particular group. Just to make this crystal clear, let me give you a couple of examples:

Ex. 1. A car is made to drive (disposition), but some operators will drive fast, slow, or reckless depending upon who is controlling the steering wheel (personality).

Ex. 2. All windows help people see outside (disposition), some windows have a blue, green, yellow, or black curtains on them (personality).

Hopefully, those two examples give you a clear understanding of the difference between disposition and personality. Nevertheless, this is all to say that there is a certain disposition that is required for each fivefold office, but the personalities that makeup fivefold offices are diverse. Sometimes, people assume that a person is of a certain office because of a personality. In other words, just because someone is extroverted, has a charismatic personality, and loves to be around people, does not automatically mean they are an evangelist. On the contrary, someone can have an introverted personality, not have a wide friendship circle, and yet, there are times where their office as the evangelist causes them to go out and meet people to share the gospel. And they do great at it even though they are an introverted personality because they are anointed to do so.

Moreover, just because someone has a serious and dogmatic decorum to their personality with a hint of anger, does not mean they are a prophet…it just might mean they are a bully! Prophets can have fun personalities, they can laugh, and still be anointed by God. Hence, the title represents a disposition, not a personality. And it will be important to keep these thoughts in mind when we begin to break down the required dispositions that validate each office.

Title Represents The Function

My father left when I was somewhere around four or five years old. And I have had little to no contact with my father for very long spans of my life. In short, I do not have a relationship with my father. On one occasion I saw him at a family gathering and as he was talking to me he started to give me advice as a father would his son. He kept telling me things I ought to do while simultaneously addressing me as "boy" authoritatively. At the time I was hearing this instruction from my father, I was already married to my beautiful wife, had children of my own, and was in my thirties…so I'm thinking to myself, "You're a little late." I was annoyed because where was all this information in my earlier years of life—"You left me!!!" I thought. Every time he called me "boy" as a breathing marker at the end of each sentence it was extremely agitating to me, as I tried to maintain my Christian demeanor and mindset.

Why were his words so irritating to me? Because title without the function is an insult. I felt insulted by his words because even though he had the title of "father" he did not function as a father throughout my entire life. When someone has a fivefold title, but there is no function, it hurts the Body of Christ.

If one claims to be an evangelist then you should be able to function as an evangelist. You should have specific and unique gifts to share the gospel and equip others to do the same. Evangelism should come naturally to you if you hold that office. If you claim to be pastor, you should be at a church somewhere nurturing and caring for God's flock, and yet, I have met those that say, "I am a pastor," but they have no flock. If you claim to be a prophet then you should be able to act prophetically and the list goes on and on. If you hold a fivefold office then you should have access to the gifts of that office and function with them.

Some people take a fivefold title without understanding its function for at least two reasons:

1. They are not called into an office but they are members of the Body who have limited gifts or functions related to an office. So they think that because they have a desire to do mission trips they should be an apostle. Or they have a preaching grace, and now think they should be a pastor of a church. In short, they get into an office that they have not been called by God to and cannot operate with all the functions.

2. They think that by claiming an office it makes it so. And even though they do not have any of the function associated with said office, they claim to hold a certain office because it makes them feel and appear powerful.

Medical doctors function like medical doctors; firefighters function like firefighters; police officers function like police officers; we know this because there is something not only in their attire that informs us of their role/office, but they also have the tools attached to their office that support the function. We often see a doctor with a stethoscope hanging around their neck, a firefighter in rubber boots or breathing apparatus, a police officer with a utility belt comprised of a gun and handcuffs. And we understand that each tool attached to these professionals represents the function they have in a given space or community. Likewise, if you have a fivefold title, you should have gifts (tools) associated with that title—there must be a function. Jesus was the Messiah not just because He and others said so—no, He functioned like it.

The Office Finds You

Becoming a fivefold minister is not something you can earn, but it's a calling. And it's a calling you do not have to look for because it finds you. We often say things like, "I'm looking for my calling," when in reality the calling presents itself to you in God's timing. Just like how we were not looking for God, but rather He came to us (Isaiah 65:1), the calling, mission, and office God has for your life will present itself to you. You just remain faithful, ask God to reveal it to you in due season, and be at peace. However, if you feel pressure and/or anxiousness to step into an office, then that is not from God.

When God called people into an office they were not straining or desperately searching for one. Moses was happy and at peace taking care of his father-in-laws' sheep when God called him. Samuel was sleeping when God called him. Elisha was not looking for a mentor but rather the Prophet Elijah presented himself to him. When Jesus called His first disciples they too were minding their own business and were happy with their trade as fishermen, but they dropped their nets and followed Jesus. The calling has a way of finding people when they are at rest, and at unexpected times.

A person must not force themselves into an office until God promotes them. I remember hearing a story of a man who excelled above his peers in one department of a company, so the higher-ups promoted him to an executive position. This man worked tirelessly at his new position. He would show up early and leave late, and his work was always excellent. One day, he gets called into his boss's office. The boss tells the man how proud he is of his work, and how he has noticed that he's willing to put in extra hours more than anyone else. So the boss decides to offer the man another position with more benefits and responsibility. At this, the man breaks down in frustration, and exclaims, "I cannot do this anymore, the only reason I have been working all these extra hours is that I can barely keep up with the workload." In short, he had to work harder and longer because he was in a position he really could not handle. And even though he was able to produce good work, the burden of his new position was too much for him to bear. Likewise, when someone steps into an office God has not given them grace for, they will just be running on pride. And as we all know they will eventually experience burnout because *"Pride goes before destruction, a haughty spirit before a fall,"* (Proverbs 16:18). Let God promote you in His time, and not anxiousness or pride.

Inner And Outer Call

Now that you have the proper understanding of the title representing a disposition and a function, it's time to talk about how one knows they have a fivefold office. No one is self-appointed into an office, rather, one will have what is called the inner and outer call. The inner call in that God personally makes it self evident to the individual that He has called them to an office. The outer call in that others recognize that you have an office typically through verbal affirmation (John 4:19), the laying on of hands (Acts 8:17), and/or anointing oil (1 Samuel 16:13). God makes sure, there is public recognition and ordination of your office.

On one occasion, Jesus asked His disciples about His reputation among the people. And then the disciples said that some thought He was the reincarnation of John the Baptist, the Prophet Elijah, Jeremiah, or some unnamed prophet. Upon hearing what the crowds had been saying, Jesus then asked His disciples about who they thought He was. And then Peter told Jesus that He was the Messiah and the Son of God (Matthew 16:13-20)! Of course, Jesus already knew who He was. His inner call was confirmed when He was a boy at the temple (Luke 2:41-52), and even at His baptism God the Father and the Holy Spirit appeared personally to affirm Jesus (Matthew 3:16-17). But there was also this outer call, a recognition given by Peter, of the role or office of Jesus as Messiah.

As we investigate the Bible, it seems to be a regular occurrence…this inner and outer call. Samuel experienced the inner call by God directly and personally reaching out to him when he was sleeping as a boy. God spoke primarily through His prophets in the Old Testament, and during Samuel's time there were not too many prophets declaring the oracles of God. So, for Samuel to hear the voice of God calling to him in his sleep meant that God was revealing to the boy Samuel that he was a prophet. However, Samuel did not realize that God was speaking to him until he received the outer call from his mentor, the Priest Eli, who affirmed his prophet status by telling him it was God calling to him in the night (1 Samuel 3).

Moses had the inner call throughout his entire life that he would be a deliverer and prophet for Israel. When he was living as an Egyptian he felt compelled to defend Hebrews. And even though at the beginning, his inclination for being a deliverer was implemented in the wrong way in that he murdered an Egyptian for his mistreatment of a Hebrew man, it was still an indication of God's inner call on his life to be a deliverer for God's people. Moses would experience the inner call more directly from God in the form of a burning bush. And then, Moses received the outer call when Moses presented himself as God's prophet and deliverer to the elders; they listened to him and it caused them to bow down and worship God (Exodus 4:29-31). Over and over again, we can see the inner and outer call. If you have an office, God will make it self evident to you and there will be others who recognize it.

More Than One Office?

As people, we usually hold many offices. I am a husband, father, son, Christian leader, etc. Likewise, it's entirely possible to have more than one office of the fivefold ministry. Typically speaking, a person will have one office in which they can fully operate in the disposition and the function of said office. Nonetheless, some people can operate in two offices. In short, a person could truly have multiple offices but no single person can hold all the offices. Why is that? Because only Jesus held all five offices while on earth. Remember, as we talked about in chapter one, Jesus **is** the Fivefold Ministry. Jesus never "had" one of the fivefold offices as we do, He **is** the Fivefold Office. But when He ascended to go back to God the Father, He distributed His Fivefold Office, into five distinct offices known as apostle, prophet, evangelist, pastor, and teacher. Therefore, if someone held all fivefold offices, they would be Jesus—and that would never happen since there is only one God, and one Savior for all. To claim or desire to have all fivefold offices, would be an attempt to remove the Lordship of Jesus Christ.

Furthermore, God does not allow an individual to hold all the offices because then we would not feel the need to be in community with other believers. We would feel self-sufficient thinking that we do not need our other brothers and sisters. But no, I need other Christians in my life to sharpen me because I do not have all the gifts (Proverbs 27:17). Christians are called to be in community with one another. In other words, I need to experience Christ in you, and you need to experience Christ in me.

One cannot not possess every office, but one may possess multiple offices. Philip was a deacon and evangelist. Deborah was a judge and prophet. Moreover, some have held three offices: David was a king, pastor, and a prophet. Samuel was a judge, prophet, and priest of Israel.

So let's say an individual holds three offices...for example, a person may truly operate with the disposition and function of a pastor, prophet, and evangelist. Basically, at times this individual has moments where they are extremely pastoral. They know how to nurture and love their congregation as Jesus would. But then there are moments where they are as a prophet, and they are pointing people to righteousness, and are supernaturally and specifically uttering the oracles of God over regions or individuals. Then, you notice that when they are in a public setting, they show a completely different disposition and function from that of pastor and prophet. The difference now is they have this passion to talk to random people about the gospel because they are acting in the office of the evangelist. You may have noticed a fivefold minster switch or change like this before, but you did not have the comprehension as you do now to know they have multiple offices. And this is not the same as having one office, and being able to use or borrow other gifts from another office when needed. No, this is a person who truly has been anointed by God to hold multiple offices. Having a minister like this can be interesting, because each encounter with this minister can be different, depending on which office God is drawing out of the minister at the time. If someone carries more than one office, it is my suggestion that it's best to go with one title so as not to confuse people. Therefore, if you have multiple offices, but you find God drawing the pastor out of you more times than not, then you should probably stick with the title pastor. However, it also might just depend on the platform. For example, at my church I am recognized as "pastor," and that is the disposition and function I typically have for my local congregation. However, when I get invited places to preach and teach, they often are calling on me as a prophet. They know that I hold the office of prophet, and they want me to arrive and operate as such. In those settings, people address me as "prophet" and not as "pastor."

I would also like to suggest that in my experience, it's rare to see someone operating in more than two offices. It's possible! But typically speaking, if you begin to notice that a minister seems to be able to function in more than two offices, it could be that they are an apostle and they may not know it yet. The calling is there but the commissioning is yet to come. In other words, they may hold the office of an apostle, and because the apostle has to be at least decent or good at the gifts of other offices, it may seem like they hold multiple offices when they only have just the one.

Can A Person Lose Their Office?

A person can lose their office because of disqualification. King Saul, was anointed to be the King of Israel, but he lost that office having sinned against God (1 Samuel 13:1-14). God is graceful and merciful. He works tirelessly in giving people opportunities to repent and do the right thing. Jonah was a prophet who did not want to share the word of God to the people of Nineveh. He thought he could escape God, but even then, God stopped him by having him swallowed up in a big fish. After Jonah repents, he does what God told him to do. What I'm trying to say, is that God is long-suffering, and will give a fivefold minister opportunity, after opportunity, to be faithful to their office. But if a fivefold minister is continually negligent in the task God has given them and continues to hurt God's people as a result, then God will strip them of their office for their own sake and the sake of those under their ministry.

And it does not necessarily mean that the person stripped of their office is condemned by God or was never a Christian. They just lost the character and commitment that was required to maintain their office. Even the Apostle Paul talked about not wanting to be disqualified in his ministry (1 Corinthians 9:27).

CHAPTER 6

THE APOSTLE

The word "apostle" in its original Greek form, is the word "apóstolos." It means "One who is sent" or "to send." All Christians are called and commissioned to share in the ministry of Jesus Christ in the world. Much like Jesus was sent by the Father, so Jesus sends us, His disciples into the world (John 20:21). Every Christian is an ambassador for Jesus and His kingdom. Nevertheless, an apostle is a specialized and uniquely gifted governmental ambassador that is sent by God to establish the revelation, purposes, and plans of God for a given region or area. They produce new advancements for the Church and are conduits of kingdom manifestation. These are true pioneers of the faith.

Yet, for many people when they think about the apostle, this is what comes to mind, "?." In other words, the apostle is a big question mark. That is to say, there are numerous Christians who have had little, to no contact with modern apostles. And as a result, they perceive the idea of modern apostles with ambiguous acceptance or skepticism about the office entirely. But, for those that have experienced the ministry of this office, you know it is very much needed in the Church and the world.

It's hard to not mention prophets when talking about apostles because they share some similarities. As the Bible says, the Church is "...*built on the foundation of the apostles and prophets..*," (Ephesians 2:20a). So what one needs to understand is that for God's kingdom and His Church to expand after Jesus ascended to the Father, there would need to be pioneers (apostles), and revelators of the mind and heart of God (prophets)—they gave the initial push for God's kingdom and Church. And they continue to make advancements for the kingdom today.

Think of the fivefold as a new start-up business. There must be an entrepreneur who has revelation and insight to seek out new territory for clients and establish the structure and order for a new base of operations (apostles). You will need a business strategist or consultant who has the same revelation, but can strategize, evaluate the plans, provide more insight, give more direction, and passion for the new start-up (prophets). Once the territory has been identified and established you now need some advertisement or good PR to continue the promotion and invitation of new clients and employees (evangelists). There will also need to be people of said business that are managers who nurture the community and culture surrounding the business...they provide recreation, comfort, and connection to the client or employees of the business (pastors). Finally, you will need the purposes, statutes, principles, and plans of said business to be restated or retaught regularly to employees and clients to keep everyone involved on task and/or to understand the purpose (teachers).

This analogy of fivefold ministry is constantly cycling throughout the Church and world—God is constantly doing a new start—increasing revelation that will require all the fivefold members to do their part, and thus, we ought not to think apostles and prophets, or any one particular fivefold member is better than the rest. In essence, God's apostles and prophets are like the foundation, studs, and/or pillars of a house or building. These weight-bearing attributes are not always visible to the naked eye. And yet, we know there are foundations under buildings, studs hidden in walls, and pillars covered up by decorations. God's not bringing back the apostles and prophets, they have always been here, maybe you just have not been able to identify them, until now.

Disposition

Kingdom-focused: Apostles are not just focused on the local congregation as a pastor would be. But rather, they have a passion to see God's kingdom expand into new territories. This insatiable desire to see God's kingdom come and His will be done, on earth as it is in heaven (Matthew 6:10), propels the apostle to see new churches established; activate and train new ministries and ministers; impart a new revelation or structure for the Church; and exhibit the kingdom manifestation of signs, wonders, and miracles. They are like the entrepreneurs of God's kingdom.

They truly believe that God's kingdom should influence everything. This is why the Apostle Paul was compelled to talk with kings and rulers like King Agrippa in the Bible. The apostle believes God's kingdom should affect business, governments, medicine, communities, commerce, the internet, and nations; you name it and the apostle wants God's kingdom to influence it. The local pastor thinks, "What's good for the church God has asked me to shepherd?" Whereas the apostle thinks, "What kingdom impact can I have on the world?" Apostles anticipate the second coming of the Kings of kings, and they want to make sure there is not just a church (a local assembly of believers) but a kingdom for Jesus to return to. The Church is what Jesus built, the kingdom is what we are to continue to establish not just in the Church but in the world—nobody understands that better than an apostle.

Suffers hardship for the kingdom of God/Church's sake: Because they are pioneers, apostles must advance the kingdom and start new Christian communities wherever God may send them. Sometimes they get a new revelation that others are not ready to receive yet, but they must continue to present God's revelation despite the costs. When Paul would speak of his new revelation of the gospel for the Gentiles, not everybody readily accepted that revelation (Galatians 2:11-21). Paul also endured great physical ailments, torment, and dire situations to advance the Church and kingdom (2 Corinthians 11:24-27).

Adequate in many aspects of ministry: Because they seek out and develop new ministries, apostles must have some level of understanding and practice in all the gifts. This is why Paul, who held the office of an apostle, was able to teach or train on different gifts and offices (1 Corinthians 12), because an apostle must be great at doing the work of an apostle (providing structure, order, training, advancements, support for other ministers, and the like), by being at least good or adequate in every aspect of ministry.

Other anointed ministers and people are drawn to them: Plain and simple, anointed people want to be around other anointed people—an apostle naturally draws gifted people around them because they can activate and train people in their gift or office. They have a magnetism or apostolic drawing like Jesus, who simply looks at fishermen, invites them to be His followers, and they drop and leave everything behind to be a disciple of Jesus (Matthew 4:18-20).

They are not easily persuaded by anything but the kingdom of God: While a local pastor may care about every single detail in a congregants life, the apostle is not shaped that way. A pastor may start family game nights, and produce messages that have to do with family life. Whereas the apostle may host activation nights of the prophetic, healing, and classes that train people in their gifts because that is their disposition and function as a minister. It's not that they do not know how to be pastorally nurturing, God has just caused them to be persuaded by the manifestation of the kingdom of God more than anything else. So if you notice that you have a "pastor" that does not focus much on youth programming, counseling, or doing weddings and funerals; it could be you have a "pastor" who is an apostle. If this is the situation, God may raise a pastor to assist the leadership of the "pastor" who is an apostle, in the area of pastoral care for the congregation.

Receive unique revelations: Whenever you listen to an apostle preach, teach, or even counsel, you might find yourself saying, "I've never heard that before." You may have read a Bible passage over and over again, but when the apostle breaks that passage down, you see things you did not before. This is because an apostle receives fresh revelation from God that is meant for the Church and the advancement of God's kingdom. The Apostle John gave us a new revelation of the end times that we call the book of "Revelation." Even the Apostle Paul spoke of the suffering he had endured for the new revelations God had given him (2 Corinthians 12:6-8).

Taught by God personally/personal examples: Apostles and prophets truly draw their strength from being in the presence of God. It's hard to imagine a true apostle or prophet not having a strong prayer life. This is not to say that other offices do not have a prayer life, it's just that apostles and prophets connect with God deeply through prayer—God does not leave their mind. The evangelist may have a deep desire to share the gospel with people, and the teacher a deep desire to study Scripture, but apostles and prophets live on the revelation of the Lord. They have to be close to Him. Therefore, many times, what an apostle or prophet learns did not come from an institution, but directly from God in prayer (Galatians 1:11-12). They may use a lot of personal examples while preaching and teaching, not because of arrogance or pride, but because God has dealt with them so personally.

Patient visionaries: The apostle can be patient in hard times and/or in their dealings with their mentees because they already see the result. They are not decent or even good mentors, they are great mentors! They do not want to rush any process and will take the time with projects and people to make sure the end result honors the Lord. The Scripture informs us that the Apostle Paul did not rush the mentorship process with his mentee, Timothy. He took the time to teach him a certain way to live as a minister of God (2 Timothy 3:10).

Walk-in spiritual authority: Apostles have swagger! They know that God has called them and will not pretend like God has not. They face the kingdom of darkness head-on, knowing the God that sent them will see them through it. To be a pioneer they must be sure of their calling and the God that sent them because they are doing new things that people will not always applaud until proven. But the apostle already knows that what they are pioneering is true because God had revealed it to them. Even if no one agrees, the apostle presses forward having the applause of heaven. So they have to be confident. Paul was never bashful in announcing who he was or what he was about in spite of opposition. Rhetorically speaking the Apostle Paul says:

> "*Am I not free? Am I not an apostle? Have I not seen Jesus our Lord? Are you not the result of my work in the Lord? Even though I may not be an apostle to others, surely I am to you! For you are the seal of my apostleship in the Lord.*" (1 Corinthians 9:1-2).

Function

Signs and wonders: The Apostle Paul said, "*I persevered in demonstrating among you the marks of a true apostle, including signs, wonders and miracles,*" (2 Corinthians 12:12). Signs and wonders follow the ministry of true apostles. They have a desire to see the lame walk, the blind see, and the dead raised. They take it personally whenever someone has an ailment, and apostles have a mindset that says, "This person ought to be healed," because the mantle of the healing ministry is deeply upon them (1 Corinthians 12:9b). Every Christian has some measure of faith (Romans 12:3), but apostles have a strong gift of faith that can move mountains (Mark 11:23, 1 Corinthians 12:9a). They practice the deliverance ministry of the casting out of demons (Luke 11:20). When an apostle is around, expect to experience the supernatural.

Trainers and activators: Teaching and training are two different subjects. There has been a lot of teaching in the Church because it's important, but there has not been enough training. Teaching gives you information, whereas training is the implementation of such teaching. Apostles love to mentor and train people. Jesus did not just teach people, but rather, He trained His disciples on how to do what He did and sent them out into the community to preach, teach, and perform signs and wonders (Luke 10:1-23). Apostles "put you in the game." They see what you are meant to become, thus they help to take what you have learned and put it into practice. They have a unique gifting in which you become activated in your faith. If you have a desire to do mission work, evangelize, perform miracles, prophesy, or even want to influence the marketplace; so long as whatever desire you have is coupled with the idea of glorifying God, the apostle has a way of activating and even training you. Apostles have a legacy on their mind. And not the kind of legacy that is based on vain conceit, but they want to have a legacy of godliness follow them. Therefore, they do not just have students, they feel like they have spiritual sons and daughters they have trained and developed that will carry on and even further what God began with them. The Apostle Paul was not just another teacher or coach in Timothy's life or the churches he established. He was like a father (1 Corinthians 4:15).

Structure and order: This is deeply rooted in the apostle. The apostle does not tolerate dysfunction and disorder! Why? Due to their pioneering spirit of establishing and developing new churches, ministries, and ministers, they understand that the sustainability and stability of all that is established must have proper structure and order. When Jesus noticed that a church was functioning more like a business than the house of God, He flipped over tables, made a whip, and drove the people that were corrupting God's house out (John 2:13-17). Noah was given specific instruction on how to build the structure of the ark and the order of how the animals were to come into the ark (Genesis 6:15-22). Likewise, the apostle sets out to maintain structure and order for God's house/kingdom. The apostle says, "do it right, or not at all."

Church discipline/correction/accountability: Here is a worthy saying, "Discipline is administered by the fivefold, accountability is administered by the body (congregation)." At this point, I have four children all under the age of nine. Imagine for a moment that I authorize my oldest son to administer discipline to his younger siblings. Just imagine me allowing my son to take things away, put in time out, and give spankings to his other siblings whenever he felt it was necessary! Hopefully, you would all say that would be wrong, because it is my responsibility as the parent to discipline my children. Ideally, as the parent, I'm the more loving, responsible, wise, and calibrated enough to know how to administer discipline correctly and effectively without bias. Nonetheless, my children can help keep their other siblings accountable. They could say in my absence, "You know dad said we shouldn't do that, so maybe we should stop."

In the same manner, it would not be healthy for everyone in God's kingdom or Church to administer discipline because not every believer is mature enough to administer discipline correctly…that is reserved for fivefold ministers. The Body can hold one another accountable. There are times when you need a loving Christian to tell you, "I think you going the wrong way, I care about you and don't want you to hurt yourself." However, fivefold ministers who exhibit the fruit of the Spirit (Galatians 5), will in a spirit of love and redemption; correct, restrict, excommunicate, and guard the kingdom of God and the Church from the wolves (2 Timothy 4:2, Matthew 7:15).

Preaching and teaching fresh revelation of the kingdom: An apostle does not just give you information, but rather, revelation and impartation. Someone in the office of the teacher is great at filling in the details and giving a bevy or buffet of information to inform your study and Christian walk. But information alone does not always produce change. People know that cigarettes are bad for them, yet they still purchase them. However, when an apostle speaks, they tend to give a revelation you have never heard before. They acquire new insight from God (which is not contradictory to the nature and plans of God already revealed in Scripture) that others begin to teach. And such revelation becomes an impartation or is conferred on you in such a way that it changes the course of direction for your life (apostles do this but prophets specialize in this). The apostle rides the wind of the new thing God is doing! They are the ones who have and do chart doctrine for the Church (Acts 2:42).

Establishment of kingdom manifestation regionally and/or globally: There is always new ground to be explored and acquired for the Lord—apostles seek it out. They are like the talent scouts, entrepreneurs, innovators, and pioneers of the kingdom. Wherever they are, they will activate something new. If you ever hear of a new church in your community where there is a new "pastor" who believes and practices signs and wonders…it could be that "pastor" is an apostle. And the community had not experienced the manifestation of God's kingdom power for a long time, so God sent an apostle to the area.

Potential Flaws

An apostle always has to be prudent to guard their heart against the sin of pride and/or arrogance. Because they receive such strong revelations from God personally, they may be tempted to feel like "super-apostles"—to be caught up in their uniqueness and vanity. The Apostle Paul says that because of the revelations he was receiving, God had to keep him from becoming conceited (2 Corinthians 12:7-9). And if their natural sense of authority is not calibrated by the fruit of the Holy Spirit, they can resemble more of a bully than a servant of God.

The Controversy

Some people have drawn the conclusion that to be an apostle one must have supernaturally seen Jesus. There are two primary Scriptures used for this argument:

> "*Therefore it is necessary to choose one of the men who have been with us the whole time the Lord Jesus was living among us, beginning from John's baptism to the time when Jesus was taken up from us. For one of these must become a witness with us of his resurrection.*" (Acts 1:21-22).

and...

> "*Am I not free? Am I not an apostle?* **Have I not seen Jesus our Lord?** *Are you not the result of my work in the Lord?*" (1 Corinthians 9:1, emphasis mine).

The context of the first passage is that the apostles were looking for someone to replace Judas. And of course, those early Christians had a recent memory of Jesus walking the earth. And with Christianity not being spread throughout the world as it is today, and the contention surrounding the life, death, burial, and resurrection of Jesus Christ; the apostles had a limited number of people (about 120) they could pull from (Acts 1:15). Those early apostles had an in-person experience with Jesus before He died, after He resurrected, and ascended. Jesus also had encountered many people besides the 12, including the 120. So the apostles just wanted to make sure that whoever would have replaced Judas, would be from that limited pool of believers who had firsthand experience with Jesus and witnessed the resurrection— these were the people that already had personal teaching and training from Jesus, and thus, made them the most qualified at the time. Having learned directly from Jesus and bearing witness to the resurrection was an early identifying mark the apostles used to qualify other apostles, but it was not a lasting mark.

This is why in our second verse Paul says rhetorically *"Have I not seen Jesus our Lord?"* Because he was using that initial qualifying mark, to validate his apostleship! Paul did not have the same experience as the first apostles did with Jesus. Paul's encounter with Jesus was in a vision (Acts 26:19), and not in the flesh or in-person like the first apostles...but he no less saw Jesus which is his argument. So in his list of reasons for why he is an apostle, he makes sure to say that I have seen Jesus just like the others. However, to base apostleship on physically or supernaturally seeing Jesus in a vision, would not continue to be an identifying mark for apostleship. Why? Because Jesus said to the Apostle Thomas who doubted His resurrection, *"'Because you have seen me, you have believed; blessed are those who have not seen and yet have believed,'"* (John 20:29). Once more, those early apostles needed to fill an immediate need (replacing Judas) and so they wanted somebody who had already proven their belief because they had sat underneath the tutelage of Jesus personally and had witnessed the resurrection—that is all!

Moreover, Scripture teaches that after Jesus ascended back to the Father, He gave gifts such as apostles, prophets, pastors, evangelists, and teachers (Ephesians 4:8-12). Notice that after Jesus left the earth, and nobody saw him, He still was establishing and sending apostles after the original 12. Apostleship is a gift received not something attained by the eyesight (2 Corinthians 5:7). Likewise, today, even though many ministers have never seen Jesus (1 Peter 1:8a), the Lord still establishes new fivefold ministers including apostles for every generation.

To base apostleship on seeing Jesus, is a fleshly matter and not a spiritual one. Moreover, we need to be careful when we consider apostleship on the bases of having seen Jesus in some bodily form. Because the Lord warned that there will be false christs who appear and say they are Jesus (Luke 21:8). No, our faith is based on the Spirit and not the flesh—that the Christian has come to experience Christ personally, and we bear witness to the resurrection, even though we did not see it like those early apostles, because the Spirit within us convinces us of this truth (1 John 5:1-9, Romans 8:15).

One may still hold to the idea that one must see Jesus to qualify as an apostle. And while I disagree, it's not a salvation issue to where we must have endless debates and call somebody a heretic. Nonetheless, apostles do have deep personal experiences with God. They have to if they are going to offer the Church a new revelation, pioneer, and perform signs and wonders. There are contemporary testimonies from Christians and apostles who have seen Jesus enter the room physically, had a vision of Jesus, a dream of Jesus meeting with them, or heard the audible voice of Jesus. If New Testament believers like Paul and Ananias could have personal encounters with the Lord post ascension (Acts 9), then us modern New Testament believers can have unique and personal experiences with the Lord before He returns. As we have now looked at the disposition and function of the apostle, hopefully, you understand what makes an apostle.

Apostolic Testimonial

I have a ministerial friend who is an apostle. He loves structure and order as any apostle does. He has told me stories of the past, both personal and second hand, of how a church can be disrupted and divided when there is not structure and order. Hence, he believes strongly that nobody should come into a church and start randomly prophesying to people in secret without letting the fivefold leadership know. And rightfully so! God has placed the visionary leader over the house to give direction for the congregation. So, unless the visionary leader has designated a person or persons to operate freely in the prophetic, nobody...whether a congregation member or visitor should be sneakingly pulling people to the side and saying, "Thus says the Lord," without consulting leadership. A prophetic word should have other witnesses to hear and see if it's from God (1 Corinthians 14:29). Because it could be a corrupted prophetic word from someone with a demonic spirit (Acts 16:16-18, 2 Corinthians 11:14).

One time while visiting the worship service of my apostolic friend. God was really moving among the service. There was such freedom of expression in the worship service. And then suddenly, I witnessed my apostolic friend correct someone first hand who tried to give a word during the service. A woman stood up to speak what the Lord was saying without consulting him, and he quickly stopped her by saying, "Ma'am, you hold onto that and we'll speak after the service."

In my early stages of Christianity, I would have thought he was quenching the Spirit from operating freely. However, imagine a random stranger walking into your house unannounced and they start telling your children what to do: "Go to your room, sweep the floor," or they start rearranging all your furniture. It would be different if this was a friend or family member who knew your expectations and with permission was assisting you. But it would be reckless, inconsiderate, chaotic, and perhaps dangerous if a stranger were to enter your house, demanding, and rearranging everything without your consent.

The same is true when somebody comes into a church that they are not submitted and committed to. Without knowing the unique mission or calling of an individual church, they come in and recklessly prophesy over the congregation God has never made them responsible for. They should check with the visionary leader of the house or those put in charge of the prophetic, before delivering the word recklessly. If it is a prophetic word from God that serves the mission of the house or its individual members, then one should have no problem asking the leadership for permission to share it.

The apostle will be quick to make sure there is structure and order to the house of God. Just like the physical body needs a structure and order to be healthy and function, the apostle knows the Body of Christ (Church) needs it as well. God is not an author of chaos and confusion but of order. So, wherever there is a well balanced and healthy church, rest assured, there must be an apostolic influence that helped maintain its integrity.

CHAPTER 7

THE PROPHET

I was listening to a sermon from Leonard Ravenhill, where he said: "...the prophets were men who walked with God, they felt like God, they saw like God, they wept like God, they yearned like God." If you are willing to accept this statement then you have conceptualized the nature of the prophet.

Prophets are the mouthpieces for God, they are God's spokesmen—they foretell and forth tell. They tap into the mind and heart (will, plans, principles, passion, etc.) of God and reveal His message to regions, communities, and individuals. There is an expression, at least in the United States, that whenever there is someone we love or we are very close to we say, "That person has my heart" or "That person is my heart." And God would say of the prophets that "They are my heart!" Prophets dwell so close to the heart of God that the prophet Amos said, *"Surely the Sovereign LORD does nothing without revealing his plan to his servants the prophets,"* (Amos 3:7).

Old Testament vs New Testament Prophets

Without a doubt, Old Testament prophets dealt with a lot of correction and condemnation. While there is grace in the Old Testament, God's full manifestation of grace was yet to be revealed in Christ Jesus. In the Old Testament disobedience got you kicked out of the Garden, turned you into a pillar of salt, and got you stoned to death; entire nations were destroyed, the earth was flooded, at times God would even distance Himself from His people Israel because His righteousness would have killed them (Exodus 33:3). Now, of course, we see a glimpse of this wrath in the New Testament. Ananias and Sapphira lie to the Holy Spirit concerning their financial offering and they drop dead suddenly—instant judgement (Acts 5:1-11). So there are instances in the New Testament where God's wrath was imposed. Nonetheless, God's judgement is reserved until Christ returns, because we are under the dispensation of grace, whereby God is giving humanity time to repent and put their trust in Jesus Christ unto salvation.

Before the Baby born in the manger, prophets were swift to proclaim God's destruction and judgement without much recourse. Jeremiah speaks of God's judgement over Israel and it happened. Noah says it's going to flood and it happens. This is why when the Prophet Samuel arrives to anoint the next king of Israel (David), the Bible says that the elders of the city shook with fear. They even asked Samuel if he came in "peace," because it was understood in the Old Testament that when a prophet showed up, it could have possibly meant they were bringing God's judgement with them (1 Samuel 16:4). However, in the New Testament, the first prophet, outside of Jesus, is John the Baptist. And while his message was at times tough, it was a message of repentance and salvation that pointed to Jesus Christ! John's message was a message of grace.

Much like John the Baptist, New Testament prophets in the modern era are called to point towards grace! Yes, prophets will still at times rebuke, renounce, and correct people as the Lord leads them. But it will be with a tongue full of grace. There will be a sense of love and desire for that person to return to God. In other words, you are not a prophet because you have a bad attitude. Love is and should be the main ingredient of any fivefold minister. And if a prophet is not loving, they are either abusing their gift or not a prophet of God.

Disposition

Burdened: God allows the prophet to share His burden for the world. Prophets can be sensitive emotionally. This is not to say they operate based on their emotions, but rather, they sense and feel the hardships of the world. Jeremiah is known as the "weeping prophet" because he witnessed the destruction he prophesied over a community. The Prophet Elisha cried out to God to resurrect the life of a widows son. The Prophet Jesus wept, at the recognition of Lazarus' death and He felt immense pain as He pleaded with the Father to remove the burden of carrying the sin of the world.

They are burdened with the message that God gives them to say—to the point that if they refuse to share the message of God it becomes painful to hold it in (Jeremiah 20:9). Prophets walk in a room, and they sense what is going on. God makes them aware of the spiritual climate. Unbeknownst to people in a room, God may be speaking to a prophet concerning an individual or situation. And God may ask the prophet to share it or it may be something for them to simply know so that they can pray for the person or situation. Some prophets get good at prophesying to people outside of the church without the person thinking it's strange. They could be behind you in the line of a grocery store, and they compliment you and/or encourage you based off of what God revealed to them about you. And you walk away feeling inspired, not realizing that the only reason that random person encouraged you is that God told them to. Prophets are extremely sensitive to what God is doing because they are burdened to share the heart of God with others.

Holiness: At times, a prophet may come across as aloof (this can be true of apostles too). Because what the prophet wants to do is hear directly from God. A prophet loves to be in the presence of God. They get lost in prayer. The word holy, literally means to be "separate." Hence, the prophet is regularly looking to separate themselves from the world, to be closer to God.

If you have a "pastor" and they do not want to attend every church dinner/potluck, are not available for your every call, or seem very "matter of fact" or "pointed" in nature—it may be that they have the disposition of a prophet. This is not to say all prophets are introverted. It just means that even if a prophet is extroverted, there will be times when they have to be with God more often than they are with people. If they are to speak the counsel of God, then they have to regularly be in His presence. And of course, any fivefold minister needs time alone with God to prepare messages and to function in their office. But for the prophet, it's different. God wants to speak through them at any time and anywhere, and so God draws them to prayer regularly. Moreover, the prophet longs to be in God's presence. The teacher may spend time in prayer with God, but they typically like to spend more time with God in study. Prophets, however, want to speak directly to God. Prophets come down the mountain like Moses, they come out of the wilderness like John the Baptist, they come out of their caves like Elijah; empowered by the presence and voice of God. They connect with God in the loneliness, in solitude. Even at times, Jesus got away from the crowd to spend time with God (Luke 5:16).

Righteousness: Prophets naturally celebrate the justice of God. They see the brokenness in the world, and perhaps within themselves, and they long to see the righteousness of God. They do not like when things or people are not morally and ethically as they should be; they are allergic to disingenuousness of any kind. Prophets believe in the purity of the Church. Prophets not only believe in the grace of God to remove the ultimate penalty of sin, but they also believe that grace can empower you to grow in righteousness (Titus 2:11-12). Prophets will not make excuses for sin. They love the presence of God, and because sin keeps us out of the presence of God, they hate it! It's not surprising that the Prophet Amos said, *"...let **justice** roll on like a river, **righteousness** like a never-failing stream,"* (Amos 5:24, emphasis mine).

Suffers on behalf of God: The apostle will suffer on behalf of the advancement of the Church and the kingdom of God. But the prophet suffers directly on behalf of God. The prophet only sees the benefit of enduring hardships so long as it glorifies God. Of course, the apostle suffering on behalf of the Church and God's kingdom also glorifies God. But the prophet suffers because they will not tolerate anyone or anything dishonoring the God they know. It would be analogous to a person dishonoring the memory of a family member you loved dearly. Elijah could not tolerate the prophets of the pagan god Baal or how Israel dishonored his God. In effect, Elijah tells his community to follow the true God alone or not at all (1 Kings 18:21). A prophet will stand up on behalf of God.

Unhinged from societal norms: Prophets tend to be different from the society they live in. Prophets often are ahead of their time. They see the future. So the things they do and say are often received with indifference until they come to pass. Prophets are eccentric. Regardless of what other people think, they have pledged allegiance to God and are willing to follow Him. In the Bible, God had prophets do strange things to demonstration His plan or will before people. One prophet ate a scroll (Ezekiel 3:3), another walked around naked (Isaiah 20:3), another laid on his side for 430 days and cooked his food over his excrement (Ezekiel 4:4-6), and another, lived in the desert eating locusts and wild honey (Matthew 3:4). The prophets were different, erratic, misfits, and peculiar; and they still are today.

Function

Word of knowledge (past or present revelation): When Jesus dealt with the woman at the well in John chapter 4, He had never met the woman before, and yet, He was able to tell her about her past and present marital status. In short, she had five husbands in the past, and the man she was living with at the time of this encounter was not her husband. She was amazed that Jesus was able to shed light on her past and present circumstances. A prophet can affirm or confirm what has already been or what is now. A person could have felt that God was asking them to forgive someone. And a prophet, without having previous knowledge of this, confirms the person's thoughts by saying, "I sense unforgiveness." This is a word of confirmation.

Word of wisdom (future revelation): Because of the impending flood of the entire earth, God gave Noah a word of wisdom. He told him exactly how to prepare and build the boat. A prophet may tell you, "You need to save your money" or "Don't go that way anymore" or "God is calling you to move to a certain place." And with the new wisdom, it drastically changes the outcome of the future. This is a word of preparation based on a negative or positive predicament.

Prophecy (edification, encouragement, and comfort): When the Israelites are in exile, the Prophet Jeremiah encourages the people to keep living fruitful lives while in captivity. He comforts them by imploring them to build homes, have children, and to pray for their captors, so that even while the Israelites are in bondage God may prosper them. He even tries to get them to envision the day when they will be brought out of captivity (Jeremiah 29:4-14). When the prophet is functioning with this gift, they are giving you the hope of a future situation you are not aware of yet, because your current circumstance says otherwise. This is not a confirming word, but something you have never thought of before. Prophecy is a word of hope for something you can become or gain in the future. Remember, David did not imagine himself as a king until the Prophet Samuel anointed him.

Discernment (revealers or exposers): The prophet is like a human lie detector. It's hard to fool someone who is in the office of a prophet. The prophet can see your character. When this gift is activated, the prophet is going to know if you are genuine or a poser. They spend most of their time with God. They are keen on the presence of God. Therefore, they can sense if God's presence is on your life or not. One may quote Scripture and talk about spiritual things, but the prophet can discern if the person standing in front of them knows God.

Discernment is when you just know, you get an impression about places, spaces, situations, and people. It's like when you walk in a room and you sense the tension…almost like you know people are upset even though it's not visible. Solomon, when talking to God about leading His people, he asked for the gift of discernment: *"So give your servant a discerning heart to govern your people and to distinguish between right and wrong. For who is able to govern this great people of yours,"* (1 Kings 3:9). This function allows the prophet to know the true nature of things. Jesus functioned this way: *"'Knowing their thoughts, Jesus said, 'Why do you entertain evil thoughts in your hearts,'"* (Matthew 9:4).

Intercession: In some ways, every fivefold minister does a form of intercession. However, the prophet is indeed a specialized intercessor. Because of their propensity for prayer, they will go directly to God on behalf of individuals, nations, and regions; and regularly make petitions. The book of Joel is essentially dedicated to the Prophet Joel interceding for God's people and Joel asking the people to join him in prayer to God for the national epidemic of locusts. Prophets were considered to be powerful in the Scripture. Hence, people could not overlook prophets, because many times when a prophet showed up it was to pronounce God's judgement or for intervention.

* *Prophets will also function in signs and wonders, and activate or anoint people into their ministry like the apostle. While these are not necessary functions to be a prophet, the Lord will use the prophet in this way.*

Potential Flaws

Prophets cannot determine the consequences of the words they speak. In other words, a prophet is only responsible for delivering the prophetic word God told them to speak. How people respond to that word may hurt the prophet. Hence, while some may celebrate prophets, many get rejected, gossiped about, tortured, or even murdered (Luke 13:34).

Elijah had to tell King Ahab that it was not going to rain in the region because of his disobedience to the Lord (1 Kings 17:1). No rain meant there was going to be a famine in the land that not only impacted those who had been disobedient but Elijah too. As a result of Elijah's prophetic word and the implications that followed, King Ahab's wife, Jezebel, wants to kill him. So Elijah, in order to avoid death, has to go into hiding, and what was Elijah going to do for food and water? As we know God did take care of Elijah throughout the drought/famine (1 Kings 17:2-6). Nonetheless, Elijah went through pain as a result of the accurate prophetic word God told him to speak.

It's because of the rejection and ridicule that prophets, if not calibrated by God's grace, can become bitter and angry. The prophet is more hopeful than people realize because they know the future is sure—God's justice will prevail and God's love and goodness will be preeminent—God is the Victorious One. Nevertheless, they are so aware of the brokenness and sin in the world that to ponder it too much, is to become infected by it. They can become like the writer of Ecclesiastes, where they view everything in the world as "meaningless," (Ecclesiastes 1:2).

Moreover, the prophet is only supposed to speak what God instructs them to speak. If a prophet is stepping outside of the will of God, they could end up speaking something from their will and not the mind or heart of God (Deuteronomy 18:22). When this happens it could be the case that the prophet is a false prophet or it could truly have been a mistake, in which the prophet needs to repent for their mishap and continue in the grace of God. What a prophet says, should never contradict the written word of God.

Types Of Prophets

Nabi: This is the Hebrew word that means "to bubble forth," like a natural spring bubbling forth, or "to utter." These types of prophets tend to hear words from God. They will get a sentence or more that comes to the forefront of their spirit and once they speak that one word, phrase, or sentence; more words tend to follow after unless the Spirit of God has finished speaking. They tend to speak rather rapidly, one word after another as the Lord leads them. They repeat what they hear the Spirit of God say. The Prophet Elisha, while he saw things in the Spirit like a seer (2 Kings 6:15-17), would also flow prophetically, one word after another like a nabi (2 Kings 3:15-19).

The nabi draws their prophetic utterances from within. In other words, the Spirit of God within them is bubbling up and ready to speak. So it appears like the nabi can operate prophetically at any moment without much strain. They typically get very specific utterances (names, dates, etc.).

Ro'eh (seer): This is the Hebrew word that means "to see." The Prophet Samuel was a ro'eh (1 Samuel 9:9). These types are they that receive visions or pictures in their spirit, and instead of repeating exact words from the Spirit like the nabi prophet, God gives them the ability to spiritually name and/or describe pictures using their own words. Therefore, a ro'eh (seer) typically does not speak at the same speed as a nabi prophet because the nabi is trying to keep up with what the Spirit is telling them to say. But rather, the ro'eh or seer will often receive a vision from the Lord and then pause for a moment and wait for God to give them the interpretation—it's usually at a slower pace. The nabi's prophetic ability bubbles forth from within and can be drawn upon like a well almost immediately. However, the ro'eh typically needs to wait for the anointing to hit them. They will spend time listening to music, meditating on God's presence, or even gain prophetic inspiration and instruction from looking at artwork/inanimate objects like Jeremiah did (Jeremiah 18:1-10), until the anointing of God comes upon them and reveals visions or pictures to interpret.

Dreamers: This one may be the most obvious. These are the ones that God speaks to vividly in dreams. They get their dreams from God, and they can interpret the dreams God gives to others. The easiest example of this would be Joseph and Daniel in the Bible who were both dreamers. Prophetic people like this typically have a notepad and pen by their bedside, ready to write down and interpret what the Lord was saying in the dream.

There are many types of prophets in the Bible. Some are scribal in that what they write down is prophetic (Habakkuk 2:2). Others are prophetic artists (Ezekiel 4:1-2), they may sculpt, paint, dance, and sing among many other forms of artistic expression. Moreover, it's important to note that we should not limit the prophetic to just one type. Some prophets may have a mixture of different types of prophetic streams. The same prophet that flows as a nabi may also get dreams. Nonetheless, this fivefold minister is needed in the church today. Let's take the shackles off of the prophet, and let them speak on behalf of God to the Church and the world.

Prophetic Testimonial

Some years ago, I was driving to a Friday night prophetic service in Ohio. As I was driving, my mind and heart were heavy as I had some serious decisions to make. I remember talking to God about all of my concerns. Toward the end of my prayer, I sang a song to affirm my trust in God. I have never been a good singer. Nonetheless, at the top of my lungs, I started singing lyrics from, "I Have Decided to Follow Jesus."

I arrived at the prophetic service and while in attendance, a minister on staff walks up to me and begins to speak the lyrics from the song, "I Have Decided to Follow Jesus." Afterwards, he told me how God was with me and everything was going to be fine. He even went into greater details about what the Lord was doing in my life. I had never met this minister before and there is no possible way he could have known I was singing that song in my car before arrival. I left that night extremely elated and confident in God.

The prophetic is a powerful gift that can empower and encourage the believer in their present-day circumstances. And yet, it's surprising that people claim to be in a relationship with God, but they do not think God speaks back to them personally. Or they do not believe God could give them a specific word through a prophet. God loves to communicate with us. God is aware of the current events in our individual lives and the world. And at times He will send a prophet to deliver a message that brings life and restoration.

CHAPTER 8

THE EVANGELIST

The evangelist is a "messenger of good news." And it's the best kind of good news—the gospel of Jesus the Christ. There is nothing more relevant or imperative in the mind of an evangelist than a loving, righteous, and benevolent God forgiving sins. Every fivefold minister loves the gospel and is ready to share it. All Christians love the gospel and should be willing and able to speak about it. For the gospel is the greatest message or revelation of the Christian faith and God's kingdom (Matthew 24:14). Nonetheless, the evangelist is that specialized minister that has the unique ability to propagate the gospel.

The evangelist is fearless in sharing the salvation story. They will find creative ways to meet people where they are and tell them about salvation. They love to retell the story of God's atoning love for humanity. When someone has an amazing experience at a movie theater, a theme park, at a restaurant, or in another country, they just can't keep it to themselves. They will post on social media about it; tell their family, friends, and co-workers about it; they will refer people to share in the same experience because in their mind it's so great! Likewise, the gospel is an experience the evangelist cannot keep to themselves. They want everyone to share in God's salvation story of humanity. The evangelist wants everybody to know, they can be saved...no one has to live apart from God, no one has to live with the guilt and shame of sin anymore due to the life, death, burial, resurrection, and ascension of Jesus Christ. They are heralds of the greatest story the world has ever witnessed and heard.

Evangelism is a form of worship to God. And the evangelist knows this better than most. In what has become known as "The Great Commission," when did Jesus ever say that we needed to save people? The answer is...an overwhelming "Never!" Jesus told His disciples and us today, to baptize and disciple people (Matthew 28:16-20). Jesus told us to be a witness (Acts 1:8). He told us to preach the gospel...that's it (Mark 16:15)! This is all to say that it is not the responsibility of the believer to save anybody, only God does that. However, it is our joy to tell the gospel, baptize, and make disciples! Whether people get saved or not, the evangelist finds joy in just telling the message. Of course, an evangelist or any Christian gets excited when someone is saved as a result of hearing the gospel. Nonetheless, is it a failure if after having preached the gospel no one gets saved? No, it's not a failure, because God was glorified. When one thinks it is their responsibility to save people, they take glory away from God because He alone is mighty to save. But, it is the Christian's joy and worship, to participate in sharing the gospel and watching God to do the saving.

Disposition

Suffers for the gospel: When the true gospel is preached believers will be in awe of it, new converts will be made, and/or some people will hate it. Why? Because to preach the gospel is to ultimately say that someone's culture, lifestyle, or mindset is wrong. And one must confess, repent, and believe in the Lord's salvation. This is why Stephen's evangelistic efforts got him stoned to death (Acts 7:54-60). The people did not want to submit to God, so they rejected God's message and His messenger. The mark of effective evangelism is not always that people must hate you as some people have been deceived to believe. No, some receive the gospel with gladness as the Eunuch did (Acts 8:26-40). Nonetheless, as it pertains to perpetuating the gospel in unreached and even treacherous places and spaces, with people that have violent imaginations, the evangelist is willing to suffer to get the message out (2 Timothy 4:5).

Loves outreach/mission: When an evangelist is present at your church, they want to know about the church's outreach programs. They want to get out into the community and share the gospel so that others can know God and become a part of the church. The pastor is different in that they feel extremely called to a local church, and while an evangelist feels called to belong to a church, they also feel called into the world. They are active and intentional witnesses, they want to train others to do likewise. They love being around other Christians, but after a while, they might get bored, because they are already saved. The evangelist has a desire to go to someplace to reach the lost.

Enthusiastic storytellers: These ministers know how to tell a story. They can make the most boring subjects sound epic. They are experts at breaking down the gospel from beginning to finish. They have rehearsed and said their testimony of salvation so many times that they know how to share it in any setting. They are flexible and effective communicators.

Non-revelatory (simplistic): Typically, the evangelist is not getting a new revelation from God unless they have some apostolic or prophetic graces/gifts in addition to their office. Some will operate with the "word of knowledge" in their evangelism encounters because it opens people up to receiving the gospel once they hear a personal prophetic word. Nevertheless, they tend to repeat the same story over and over again, make use of gospel tracts, or get a revelation from an apostle or prophet and use it in their evangelistic effort to inspire people. Ultimately, they want to present a clear, concise, and simplistic gospel message.

Desires to be around people: The evangelist can come across as very social. Typically speaking they want to be around people in general, but specifically speaking they want to be around sinful people to share the gospel. Jesus the evangelist, entertained the company of sinners. Why? Because He wanted to save them. So do not be surprised if you notice an evangelist wanting to be around sinful people that others have rejected. Because they know that a loving God will receive the rejected if they hear and embrace the message. And this does not mean all evangelists are extroverted. You could have an introverted evangelist that does not care to be around too many people, and yet, their office makes them want to get around people to share the gospel.

Burdened to win the lost: "Somebody needs to hear the gospel" is the thought that is always parading around in the evangelist's mind. It bothers them that people do not know how wonderful God is. They are in love with Jesus Christ, and the idea that others do not know Him causes them to stay up late, praying for people to come to a salvation knowledge of Christ.

Bold, daring, and eager: They will evangelize at the grocery store, coffee shop, movie theaters, arenas, elevators, college campuses, through social media, on the phone, and a litany of mediums the typical Christian might not think about. They know the God they serve. They know they serve the King of all kings (Revelation 19:16). Therefore, they are no respecters of persons and understand that no one is greater than the gospel. Hence, if given the opportunity, they would not be intimidated in the least to share the gospel, with any president, prime minister, king, queen, or any authority on the planet.

Function

Spiritual fishermen: They are experts at getting into conversations to share the gospel and train others to do the same —this is their primary function. They create the opportunity for the Holy Spirit to do work on someone's heart. If a person was not open to the gospel before, an evangelist will find a way to communicate effectively to them. Just like different bait is required for different fish, so the evangelist, under the inspiration of the Holy Spirit, uses different communication tools to reach people. In short, the evangelist is in the business of making the Lord's name famous. And they love to equip and train people to do the same.

A catalyst of joy /impartation of joy: To a person who refuses to submit to the Lordship of Christ, they are repulsed by the evangelist. But when a person receives and accepts the message from an evangelist, it often increases joy in their life. Why? Because naturally, anybody would be excited to know the love of Jesus Christ and that they are no longer destined for hell. Even when they are not speaking to sinners for the sake of God's glory, the evangelist refreshes and reenergizes believers of their joy for salvation and God! They have such an enthusiastic view of God that it becomes contagious.

When Jesus entered the city called Jericho, there was a tax collector by the name of Zacchaeus who was present among the crowd. Zacchaeus was despised by many of his fellow Jewish countrymen because he worked for the Roman Empire. However, Jesus decided to spend time with him at his home. The result was Zacchaeus being saved, and he had so much joy that he gave back the money he had stolen from the people (Luke 19:8). Joy was a deposit of an evangelistic encounter.

* In the following are other functions the evangelist may operate in strongly but are not required to validate their office:

Signs & wonders: When I was in college, I volunteered for campus ministry as an evangelist. My ministry was to check on my peers in the dorm halls by inviting them to chapel services, praying, and sharing the gospel with them. One of my peers opened the door and when I asked if there was anything I could pray for him about, he said, "Yes, my back is hurting." I asked boldly for God to heal his back, and it happened. He was stunned that God had healed him, so he allowed me to tell him more about Jesus.

God healing the man aided my evangelistic efforts. He experienced God's loves through healing, which led him to ask about a relationship with Christ. While the evangelist's primary goal is to share the gospel, signs and wonders is a gift that can be used to open the conversation to the gospel or even show God's love to an individual. "*So Paul and Barnabas spent considerable time there, speaking boldly for the Lord, who confirmed the message of his grace by enabling them to perform signs and wonders,*" (Acts 14:3).

Word of knowledge: An evangelist may function strongly with the gift of the word of knowledge (this gift was also talked about in chapter seven under the heading "Function"). This prophetic gift having to do with unveiling a past or present circumstance of a person's life. After Jesus revealed to the woman at the well that He knew her tragic past and present relationships with men, she became more open to hearing the truth about God from Jesus. As a result, she went back to her community and became a witness for Jesus (John 4:16-30).

The evangelist meets random people regularly while sharing the gospel. But the office of the pastor has reoccurring meetings with the people they minister to. From these regular encounters, the pastor fellowships with their congregation consistently enough to know some details about a congregant's life to better minister to them. However, the evangelist does not have that luxury. They may get one fleeting moment with a person to tell them about the gospel. Hence, using the gift of the word of knowledge helps remove some of the distance between them and the stranger. Because whether the evangelist communicates what was unveiled vocally or not, the evangelist knows something about an individual's life they can use to open the person up to the gospel message.

Potential Flaws

Because they have such a desire to get out into the community, sometimes they do not make church a priority. They become "illegal ministers," meaning that one only has authority if they are under authority...but some evangelists refuse to be under the authority of a local church. Timothy had Paul and Elisha had Elijah. All ministers must have accountability to a spiritual authority or they just become renegades working on their own strength. In particular, we are all called to be a part of a local body of believers and we draw our credibility and are rejuvenated from the local church (Hebrews 10:25). Eventually, if an evangelist or any minister/Christian, does not submit and participate in a local body, they become a church unto themselves. Where the only thoughts about God and ministry that matters most are their own. They become very narcissistic even though they claim to be doing everything for the Lord. What matters most to them is what they are doing, and they will dominate conversations with their "famous" and "great" exploits for the Lord that no one else seems to be doing. However, if one cares about what the Lord has to say, then they would make the church a priority since the Lord is pro church (Acts 2:42). They become hypocritical, as they are asking people to accept Jesus Christ and join a church, and yet, they do not make church attendance a priority for themselves.

Reaching the lost can become a replacement for personal Scripture reading and prayer. They will pray and have memorized plenty of Scripture for the lost, but they do not read Scripture and pray for their devotion and instruction. And if not calibrated by grace, they present an unbalanced gospel, where they emphasize and even enjoy talking about people going to hell with very little emphasis on God's love for humanity. Hence, their communication strength can be turned into weakness in that they win the argument but lose relationships (there are also cases where the emphasis is love with little emphasis on hell). Nonetheless, the evangelist can become unbalanced in their delivery of the gospel.

Evangelistic Testimonial

When I was in high school, I was in the locker room preparing for gym class. I remember hearing three peers talk about their Baptist church—what they liked and did not like about it. But even though they were talking about their experience, I had this sense that God wanted me to witness to them. So I said, jokingly, "You guys don't know anything about God." They gathered around me and said, "And you do?" "Yes, I do." I began to talk about Jesus Christ and His gospel. As the conversation ensued, it became apparent that while they attended church they did not fully submit their lives to Christ.

Two of my peers ended up leaving the conversation, while one remained and was glued to what I was saying. Eventually, something interesting happened. I could sense the presence of God, when all of a sudden this guy listening to me, unzipped his backpack, pulled out two pornographic magazines, and threw them into the trash. In shock, I say, "What were those doing in your backpack?" He said, "I didn't want my mom to find them at home." Something I said to him about Christ, became so attractive that he threw away his sin in his backpack, and from that day forward he would look for me at school to tell him more about Christ.

Interestingly, all of a sudden he disappeared from school. He had been following me around for weeks wanting me to disciple him. And I had no idea where he had gone, and then I never saw him again. However, about three years later, I had already graduated from high school, and I am at the public library. The same kid that I had shared my faith with three years earlier approached me. He hugged me, and said, "When you shared Jesus with me in the locker room that day, I was suicidal, I was thinking about killing myself, but because of what you did my life has changed. I'm now a youth leader at my church and I'm getting ready to go on a mission trip."

The evangelist loves moments like this! They understand that by sharing the gospel, it is just like sowing a seed. A seed does not produce overnight, but eventually it will bud. Thank God for the gift of evangelism and the evangelist who wields it.

CHAPTER 9

THE PASTOR

This is the fivefold minister we have the most experience with in our churches. Even the secular world has an idea of what a pastor does. And yet, I believe this minister is one of the most misconstrued ministers of the fivefold. It's not that we do not have some understanding of the pastor...we do. It's just that the criteria we use to determine what makes for a good pastor, oftentimes applies to the other ministers of the fivefold. In so doing, we misjudge the pastor's capability and/or commitment to excellence.

There are good and faithful pastors who question their calling because they have never been taught on the fivefold ministry. Hence, they do not know the specifics of what validates their office. So they are trying to do the work of an apostle, prophet, evangelist, and teacher; while holding their office as a pastor.

Some churches will complain, stating that the pastor is not evangelistic enough, but could it be that the lack of outreach or evangelistic zeal is because that minister is a pastor and not the evangelist? Of course, all fivefold ministers love to witness and share the gospel. However, if you expect the pastor to have the exact zeal of an evangelist; the administrative oversight of an apostle; the prophetic edge of a prophet; and the deep expository discourse of a teacher; then you have misevaluated the pastor. Unless God gives the pastor some of the gifts/graces of the other offices, then all the pastor is required to do is fulfill the role of their office.

Simply put, the title of pastor means "shepherd." What a shepherd does is take care of sheep. They guide and feed them. In essence, the pastor is a caretaker of God's sheep/congregation. Jesus referred to Himself as a pastor/shepherd

(John 10:14). My prayer is that as we delve into this office, Christians and pastors would begin to have a proper understanding of the responsibility of this office.

Disposition

A love for people: The pastor is great at exemplifying the love of God for people. Whereas an apostle may think of the church as the Lord's army to be equipped, and the teacher may see it as a class to teach, the pastor thinks of the church as a family. And rightly so! God causes the pastor to have a loving heart towards His people. The pastor always thinks they have the best church. Why? Because they love their congregation. When you are around a true pastor, you will sense that they care for you, personally. At times when you are unlovable, and you know it, the pastor will still have grace for you. This does not mean they will be a pushover. No, the pastor can still have some grit while in their office. After all, they are called to protect the flock from wolves (Matthew 7:15).

Cares about the details of your life: Your life matters to the pastor and all aspects of it. A church will feel like a family when you are around the pastor. This minister is at their best when visiting you at the hospital, at your home, supporting your event, or sitting down and sharing a meal with you as Jesus did with His disciples (John 21:12).

The other fivefold ministers may not feel as fulfilled as the pastor does to come visit you in your home due to their differing disposition and function. In fact, if your minister does not seem to have much of a desire to do visitations, funerals, or weddings; it could be because their primary office is not the pastor. But if you have not been taught the different dispositions and functions of the fivefold, you may think said minister is not as caring or compassionate, because they do not make regular phone calls or do home visitation—that is typically what the pastor is called to do. The other fivefold are caring and compassionate, it's just expressed in a way that is representative of their unique office.

Committed to the local congregation: They do not feel called to everybody like the evangelist, but rather, they feel called to the local congregation. They typically do not have a desire to preach elsewhere outside of their church. They have made a commitment to their congregation. Pastors are usually attracted to evangelists and teachers because they immediately impact their congregation in that the evangelist brings in more people for the pastor to shepherd and the teacher assists the pastor in teaching the congregation.

Suffers for the local church: The pastor loves the church so much that oftentimes they will do without so the congregation can have more. Meaning that I have known of pastors who have taken significant pay cuts to their salary so the church can afford a building, programs, and the like. Some pastors have missed birthdays, dinner time, or even sleep; to be with their congregation at their time of need. A pastor needs to create boundaries and patterns for success otherwise they can become unhealthy if they do not take time and care for themselves. Nonetheless, this is what they are called to do. They will suffer on behalf of the congregation Christ has called them to serve.

They see the finished person: Jesus saw the best in Peter even though he made many mistakes. Peter tried to keep Jesus from His mission; Peter had ideas that did not benefit the purpose of many situations: he cut off a man's ear, cursed, and denied Jesus three times. And yet, in spite of all his flaws, Christ was patient with him. Because Jesus knew that Peter would become a great leader, which he did. Likewise, when you see yourself at your worst, the pastor will still see what you can become. And the pastor will work hard to see you become all that Christ has called you to be.

Natural caretakers: Not only does church or being around the presence of a pastor feel like family, but it can also feel like a hospital or community center. They want to take care of the whole person. Like a good nurse or doctor, they have a good bedside manner. And they know how to speak to people that are hurting. At their core, they desire to see other human beings flourish in all aspects of life.

Function

Counselors: Generally speaking, it is usually favorable to run ideas by pastors because they are wise. They have overall wisdom like King Solomon and are willing and able to sit down to discuss matters with you. Even if they do not have an answer immediately, the pastor will work to find the right answer. This is when the gifting of this office really begins to shine. They know what to say, how to say it, and what will produce the best result in your life.

The apostle wants to talk about the manifestation of the kingdom, the prophet wants to talk about the heart of God, the evangelist wants to talk about the gospel, and the teacher wants to talk about the nuances of Scripture, but the pastor wants to talk about the details of your life. With Christlikeness, they want to comfort, encourage, and educate concerning matters of your life. Hence, counseling is where the pastor tends to do the most teaching. In other words, the teacher will teach through obvious pedagogy (methods or tools of teaching). However, the pastor teaches through counseling...simple but powerful and tailored advice to the person with whom they are talking. Furthermore, the pastor knows when you just need a listening ear. They have an anointed, non-anxious presence that calms.

The Apostle John experienced the comforting presence of Jesus as pastor as he rested his head upon Jesus' chest (John 13:23).

Routinely modeling Christlikeness: When you are around a pastor it may feel like you are sitting with Jesus at the communion table or at the wedding at Canaan. The pastor enjoys fellowship in your presence. The pastor is always there to be an example to the flock of Christlikeness. One may have different prophets, evangelists, apostles, and teachers come through their life. But ideally, the pastor is the one who is available for the congregation consistently.

Supports and places you in your ministry: Pastors uniquely support you in your Christian life and your calling. They know that your life will flourish as you connect with what God has designed for you. They have been in regular fellowship with you, praying for you, and asking God about your calling for a long time. Therefore, they are eager to mentor, coach, or even connect you with the ministers that can equip you.

Prayer: Every fivefold minister should be a person of prayer. But as stated in previous chapters, the fivefold minister that is really inclined to prayer is the prophet—prophets must have a strong devotional/prayer life. Nonetheless, the pastor also must be an avid minister of prayer if they are to properly take care of God's people. The pastor prays over the congregation differently than the other fivefold ministers in that the prayer of a pastor is holistic. They pray for all those little details they know about from having spent so much time with the congregation. The pastor can be counted on to pray on behalf of the congregation not only for the big things but the regular day to day aspects of the congregation's life. Ask your pastor to pray for you; they want to!

Potential Flaws

The pastor has to be careful not to become too emotionally enmeshed in the congregation. If the pastor does not practice good boundaries between themselves and the congregation, they might linger with the burdens of the congregation for too long. And they begin to take things too personally and act out sinfully. Moses became so enmeshed with his congregation that he began to complain like them. David got so enmeshed with his congregation that he had inappropriate relations with Bathsheba and murdered her husband Uriah.

In their effort to care for the flock and keep unity in the church pastors might become co-dependent. Meaning they are more inclined toward getting their congregation's approval over God's approval. In so doing, they become people pleasers instead of God pleasers. And may even refuse to correct people in their sin for fear of them leaving the congregation.

The pastor wants the best for the congregation and will work exhaustively for them. As a result, sometimes they can do too much. They take ministry that should belong to others of the congregation (E.g., they do announcements, youth ministry, clean the church, etc., when really somebody else who has time and energy might do a better job). A church can even become an idol for the pastor, where they are so busy taking care of the church, that they do not have much time for their personal relationship with God, their family, or self-care. The pastor can become highly overwhelmed and discouraged by the self-imposed duties and stress that comes with said commitment.

Pastoral Testimonial

I know of a pastor who had a congregation member who had cancer. This member had gotten so sick that he could no longer be physically at church on Sunday mornings. So about every other Sunday, the pastor would visit this congregation member at his home. He would share snippets of the previous sermons, swap stories, laugh, and pray with this member. This pastor was relentless in calling and visiting this member on a regular schedule. The wife of the sick member would occasionally be in attendance on Sundays without her sick husband, and would tell the pastor how much she and her husband appreciated the visits.

On an Easter Sunday, this beloved member died at his home. As the story has it, the pastor had just finished his Easter message. And only being home for 45 minutes after the service he gets a call stating that his member had passed away. At this point, the pastor had already undressed from his Easter Sunday clothes and was in his pajamas. But he put his dress clothes back on and immediately drove to the home of the deceased. Upon arrival, he stayed calm as he consoled the entire family who had just lost their loved one. The next couple of days he continued to calm the families hearts as he prepared to do the funeral.

After the funeral, this same pastor would then go weeks counseling the deceased wife and family. The member who had died was a farmer, and the wife was selling some of his equipment. However, she was struggling to manage her other affairs and get some of the farm equipment cleaned up to be sold. Particularly, she had a truck that needed to be cleaned up because in a few days someone was coming to buy it. Upon hearing this, the pastor decided to go over to her farm and clean up the truck for her late husband.

I bring up this story to highlight the impact the pastor had on this family. He loved the entire family throughout the process. He called, visited, counseled, comforted, prayed, and ultimately loved the one that died and his family. Even after the member had died the pastor continued to extend himself for the deceased member's family. Now, not every pastor will do exactly what was described in this story. All pastors are different. Nevertheless, the essence of this office is captured in this story.

This family did not need an apostle, prophet, evangelist, or the teacher during a time of loss. They needed God's specialized caretaker—the pastor. Hopefully, you understand why it's a misnomer to judge a pastor based on how well they preach, how well they are with administrative duties, or whether or not they are good at outreach/evangelism; while a pastor can have some of those graces, those actually are qualifications of other offices.

Several weeks after the family had time to process and heal from the death of their loved one, the wife approached the pastor on Sunday morning. And she told him how his consistent presence and love for her family meant a lot. She even went on to tell him that one of her family members who did not believe in God before, was now contemplating Christ, because of his shining example of Christlikeness. What a treasure the pastor is —they are able to love you through your greatest need.

CHAPTER 10

THE TEACHER

Herein is the fivefold minister that does not take that much to define. We all have had teachers in our lives—simply put, the teacher teaches you what you need to know about the faith. They are conduits and depositors of the truth of the Christian experience. However, there are Christian circles that have tried to blend the teacher into all of the fivefold offices. As if to say there is no such thing as the office of teacher in and of itself. But I beg to differ.

The assumption that one makes is that because the other four offices have some element of teaching, then that must mean it is not a specific office. And yes, there are some ways in which the office of apostle, prophet, evangelist, and pastor will educate you like a teacher. But it's no different in that at times the teacher can come across as evangelistic, pastoral, etc. while operating in their teaching office. In other words, all the offices have some similarities and yet they are distinct. Much like the Godhead/Trinity has similarities in that they are one, and yet distinct in three persons. So the fivefold is fantastically similar and uniquely distinct.

If I were to put the teacher's mission in a statement, it would be this: "This is what we have believed!" That is to say, the teacher is trying to define something already present. They are maintaining the Church's foundation established by the apostles and prophets, by reenforcing the history, and/or beliefs that have already been fixed in the Christian Church. They are equipped to teach in a way that promotes learning. They have mastered many or particular subjects and are armed with facts and the possible good or bad outcome of the evidence presented. The way they extrapolate a text with joy and excitement encourages knowledgable growth to those who receive the teacher.

The teacher is more educator than a revelator. Apostles and prophets are the great revelators of the kingdom. They spend time with God and get a new revelation the Church has never heard otherwise. Unlike the apostle or prophet, the teacher typically does not operate with new revelation (some are graced to). But will get a new revelation from an apostle or prophet, and then attempt to clarify the revelation so the rest of the Church can understand it.

We see the office of teacher operating in Luke's life when he wants to bring clarification to what has already been revealed. He says:

> "*Many have undertaken to draw up an account of the things that have been **fulfilled** among us, just as they were **handed down** to us by those who from the first were eyewitnesses and servants of the word. With this in mind, since I myself have **carefully investigated** everything from the beginning, I too decided to write an orderly account for you, most excellent Theophilus, so that you may know the **certainty** of the things you have been **taught**.*" (Luke 1:1-4, emphasis mine)

Luke, the great doctor and teacher, sets out to investigate what has already been "fulfilled" and "handed down," so that people could have better clarity that would give them the "certainty" of what has been "taught." This is exactly what the teacher does—reiterating and clarifying revelation as to create comprehension. This is why there have been so many teachers attempting to explain John's revelation that has become known as the book of Revelation. John had a new vision for God's people, and many teachers have had the arduous task of trying to explain what John saw in his revelation.

More Logos Than Rhema

By way of further explanation of what has already been said about the teacher in regards to not being revelatory, it's important to understand the difference between the Greek words "logos" and "rhema." The logos is the objective timeless written word of God that we have in a collection of books better known as the Bible. From Genesis to Revelation we have God's mind, heart, and will for creation. The Bible is a more than sufficient resource of who our God is and His desires. From the logos, we gain timeless truth that all must adhere to, such as the greatest commandment of loving God and your neighbor (Mark 12:30-31).

However, the rhema word is the subjective, personal, and present-day word of God to you or a specific region that does not contradict the logos (written word) of God. For example, the logos reveals to us that God does use subjective and present-day rhema words for individuals. Such is the time when God gave Philip a rhema word of needing to stand by a chariot to share the gospel with a eunuch. The interpretive logos in this narrative is that all Christians should be willing to share the gospel at all times just like Philip, but the rhema is that God told Philip specifically, during his present-day circumstance to go stand by a chariot (Acts 8:29).

So just because God personally told Philip to stand by a chariot, does not mean all Christians should stand by chariots or cars to do evangelism. Moreover, there was a subjective present-day rhema word nationally for the Ninevites delivered by Jonah concerning impending destruction (Jonah 3:1-10). However, the timeless interpretive logos is that if all people do not repent of their sins they will face destruction.

In short, the teacher operates more by the logos, than the present-day revelation of this current age we live in. The teacher is like an archeologist. Someone gets the revelation that there is a fossil or bones present in the ground. But then the archeologist (teacher) begins to clean up the fossil/bones to give us a clearer picture.

Disposition

Suffers for Christian education: The teacher despises faulty interpretations of Scripture. They love the truth, and a faulty or even slightly inaccurate interpretation of a text will bother them. Context matters, the original language matters, historical commentary on the Scripture and how the Church should operate matters. They hold hard and fast to Jesus' words of the truth making people free (John 8:32). Even the details of Scripture that are not a matter of salvation, matter to the teacher. The teacher longs to understand the truth, no matter the significance of the subject they are extremely loyal to finding the truth about it.

The evangelist and the prophet often care about getting the big picture across. "Give your life to Christ," the evangelist says. "Live holy since God is holy," the prophet says. And while the evangelist and prophet do delve into an explanation on the "why" and "how" of their statements made, the teacher will scrutinize and extrapolate their statements or observations in greater detail.

Enjoys learning: They digest many books, podcasts, blogs, and biblical commentaries. If you want to see a teacher perk up, just say you got your interpretation from the original language of the Bible. They love the source material. They tend to be good listeners because all the details matter to the teacher—they pay attention to everything. They understand that more knowledge about Christian life can only lead to a more satisfying, flourishing, devotional, and faithful life with God. Therefore, while the teacher enjoys connecting with God through prayer, church, and devotional reading, they feel even closer to God in their studies.

Technical thinkers: Like the teacher, the apostle is also a systematic thinker, especially when it comes to doctrine, structure, and order of a church. And in some ways, the teacher is a systematic thinker with the nuance being that they are more technical. The teacher wants everything to line up, and be organized. The sequence of steps or logical progression matters to the teacher. They have a scholarly approach. An apostle may release a new revelation without the sequence of steps. For example, observe how the Apostle Paul talks about a man who visited the third heaven:

> *"I know a man in Christ who fourteen years ago was caught up to the third heaven. Whether it was in the body or out of the body I do not know—God knows. And I know that this man—whether in the body or apart from the body I do not know, but God knows— was caught up to paradise and heard inexpressible things, things that no one is permitted to tell."* (2 Corinthians 12:2-4)

Notice how the Apostle Paul was uncertain about the particulars of said man's visitation to heaven. He does not give a name for the man, he does not know if it was a vision or if the man's spirit left his body, and he does not explain what the third heaven is; but all he knows is that the event did happen! Whereas for those technical thinkers such as the teacher, they concern themselves with those details. Their minds begin to churn over thoughts like, "Who is the man Paul is talking about?" "Was it a vision or not?" And, "What is this third heaven talk?" It's like when one untangles a rope or wires that have been tied together. The teacher attempts to untangle the mysteries of God's truth.

Teachable: Given that they hold the office "teacher," it is accurate to describe them as teachable. They love to take in new revelation or information. They ask a lot of questions, and if one does not recognize they are interacting with a teacher, one might think the teacher is attempting to question their authority. When in actuality, their teachable spirit is asking questions for the sake of their learning. Now obviously, some people have a "questioning spirit" and not a "teachable spirit." So they only ask questions to derail, disrupt, and disturb you. However, the teacher asks spiritual and theological questions to deepen their relationship with God.

Loves God's word: They love to have their minds stimulated by God's word. The apostle might establish doctrine, but the teacher loves the breaking down of doctrine. They are brilliant thinkers. They see in multiple dimensions and different facets. Hence, the Bible is like the greatest puzzle for them to put together. They like connecting different scriptural themes, bringing together the concepts of the Old and New Testament, and exploring the historical context of a given passage.

Function

Ability to make tough subjects plain and bring greater depth: Teachers have this great ability to open up possibilities concerning biblical or Christian truth. The teacher knows that truth makes one free (John 8:32). They know that people face hardship because of a lack of knowledge (Hosea 4:6). Therefore, the teacher works tirelessly to make learning easier for you. They will teach to your level of understanding. Whereas the prophet is more likely to say, "Either you get it or you don't, repent!"

Paul says, *"Brothers and sisters, I could not address you as people who live by the Spirit but as people who are still worldly—mere infants in Christ. I gave you milk, not solid food, for you were not yet ready for it. Indeed, you are still not ready. You are still worldly,"* (1 Corinthians 3:1-3). Paul taught them as children because that was their level of spiritual maturity. The teacher knows how to give you the information needed for the current season or maturity of your life.

Provide edifying information: The office of the teacher is essential to the Church in their own capacity, but teachers are the easiest to blend with or complement the other offices because the Church is not that apprehensive to the office of teacher. They can take what the other offices do, and add good, solid, biblical exegesis to it. This is not to say the other offices cannot teach or use biblical exegesis to aid in their ministry, but rather, the teacher can take a new spiritual revelation from an apostle, and polish the subject with its historical, and biblical context. As the Bible teaches, *"There is nothing new under the sun,"* (Ecclesiastes 1:9). So when an apostle gets a new revelation, it was already present in the Scripture, it's just that God opened the spiritual eyes to receive what we would call a new or fresh revelation. And then, the teacher further explains said revelation. In essence, it's always good to talk with any teacher about subjects of the Christian faith—you will certainly walk away having greater clarity. It does need to be said that while a teacher does bring clarity to Christian truths, sometimes the teacher has so much maturity and depth concerning a subject that they have a hard time explaining it to newer converts and immature Christians. Some teachers have so progressed in their understanding that they only know how to teach people of higher spiritual maturity.

Teaching you into correction (truth dealers): Paul said, *"Now eagerly desire the greater gifts. And yet I will show you the most excellent way,"* (1 Corinthians 12:31). The teacher is the encapsulation of Paul's statement. They want to show you what is "excellent." When what you are doing in life is not excellent, the teacher believes it's because you lack some type of knowledge. And if you permit them to teach you, they believe they can turn your reckless ideas into an excellent idea. No one is more apt to prescribing correction more than the apostles or prophets. Nonetheless, the teacher goes about correcting you by interacting with the procession of your thoughts—attempting to help the process of renewing your mind (Romans 12:2). When the visionary leader of your church is the teacher, prepare for deep and well thought out sermons and Bible studies.

Potential Flaws

When the teacher begins to operate outside of the grace given to them, they can begin to love the written word of God, more than the Jesus who is the "Word." Jesus said it best in John's Gospel while speaking to religious leaders, *"You study the Scriptures diligently because you think that in them you have eternal life. These are the very Scriptures that testify about me,"* (John 5:39). Certain Pharisees and religious leaders were constantly in opposition towards Jesus concerning matters of the Scripture, not realizing that Jesus is the true "Word" of God. He is the "Word" enacted in the flesh, He is the author of it, and the very embodiment of it. These religious leaders loved the Scripture on the scroll more than its author—Jesus Christ. Therefore, they were more concerned about doing everything right in the Scripture, than allowing Scripture to draw them into a deep admiration and love for Jesus Christ.

Likewise, the teacher can become legalistic and self-righteous, relying more on the rudiments and knowledge of their study than God to impact their lives. In other words, some things cannot be explained. And at times, if they cannot understand they will not believe it. But true faith is believing and trusting even when you do not fully understand or see. But when the teacher is at their worst, they can overly rely on and even teach that knowledge in and of itself is power. No, biblical or Christian knowledge should lead to a place of greater surrender to Christ. And therein lies the power of the Christian faith—surrendering to Jesus and the power of the Holy Spirit.

But when knowledge just puffs us up to make one feel mightier than others and to not truly surrender to God in Christ Jesus, we miss the purpose of our study. The teacher's knowledge can puff up oneself instead of building up a greater relationship with Christ. The deception is that they confuse "knowing" for "doing." James said, "*Do not merely listen to the word, and so deceive yourselves. Do what it says,*" (James 1:22).

Teacher Testimonial

I went to a Christian university with a professor that I affectionately referred to as "The Professor." In my opinion, there was no greater professor than him. He is no longer teaching at my alma mater, but in my mind, there has never been a professor like him.

What made him so great is his ability to make the most complex subjects accessible to me. Perhaps for others, readings from philosophers and/or theologians like Thomas Aquinas, Paul Tillich, David Hume, Alvin Plantinga, Anselm, Boethius, and the like; came easy to them. But some of their writings were too dense for me to understand, until "The Professor" explained it to me in the unique way he could. He was truly a gifted teacher. He fantastically held that office with all of its functions.

The teacher is such a widely accepted and needed office in the Church because they explain the truths of the faith that have become so precious to us over the years. Those deep theological and doctrinal truths such as repentance, justification, regeneration, sanctification, and the like, have been made so clear to believers because of the work of the teacher. May The Church continue to push back the darkness with the power of God's truth. God's truth is everlasting.

CHAPTER 11

APPLYING THE FIVEFOLD TO YOUR CONTEXT

I do not know how God will use the content of this book in your life. You could already be a fivefold minister and this book has added to your knowledge or clarity. You could be wondering if you are a fivefold minister. Or even be asking, "How do I make my church a reflection of fivefold ministry?" Nonetheless, my goal was to bring an understanding of fivefold ministry to people of various backgrounds. In short, the Church of the Lord Jesus Christ, and the advancement of His kingdom in the world will be of a greater impact if we accept, embrace, and practice fivefold ministry.

My caution to the reader is to not turn the fivefold into an idol in which we desire to have an office, or for our churches to be recognized as fivefold more than our connection with Jesus. In other words, the fivefold ministry is not the apex of ministry, but rather, Jesus is! Some churches base their importance on who their apostle or founding father is, if they do a certain amount of social justice, if someone was physically healed, or how big their facility is. An individual or entity could be basing their success on many things and not have a true passion for Jesus. It's possible to have ministerial success and not be faithful to Christ. Hence, the apex of your ministry is when its people and leaders, have a true, biblical, righteous, loving, and holy passion for the Lord Jesus Christ…He is the Head of the Church.

The greatest title one can ever receive is not "apostle" or "prophet," or the like, but "child of God." Before someone is recognized as a fivefold minister—whether they be an apostle, prophet, evangelist, pastor, or teacher—one must first be recognized as God's child! Therefore, if I were not a fivefold minister, I would still belong to a church, pray, fast, read

Scripture, give, and serve. Why? Because I am a child of God, this is who I am, this is what the Christian does. A fivefold title is a function one has for the Body of Christ, but who you are is God's child. One already has significance for being God's heir (Romans 8:17). How unfortunate it is when one bases their significance with God, due to their denomination, association, title, and so forth. We should feel important because even though we have sinned against God, He saved us, and now we get to have a dynamic relationship with Him. And yes, without a doubt some people are greater in the kingdom of God because of their level of obedience as Jesus stated (Matthew 5:19).

But such greatness or level of obedience cannot be determined by office or title. One could be a deacon, an elder, or a Christian without a ministerial title, but they have great obedience to what the Lord tells them to do. And that is what makes them great in the kingdom of God. Please do not turn the fivefold into an idol of achievement. The child of God just needs to be obedient to the person God is calling them to be. Now having articulated this caution, let us move on to some practical application.

Stepping Into Your Office

I talked about being called into an office earlier by way of description, but now I will talk about this by way of admonishment or caution. Perhaps one of the reasons you have read this book is because you are sensing that God is calling you into a fivefold office. God may have revealed to you what office you hold, and you already display the disposition and the function of said office. But it has yet to be recognized within a church setting or by others. Here are a few pieces of advice I want to say to you:

This is serious:

Fivefold ministers have to stand before God for every prophetic word, sermon, book, advice, and spiritual impartation they administer (James 3:1). You need to be assured that God has truly called you into an office because you will give an account to God one day. If becoming a fivefold minister is about the pride of you trying to prove something, rebellion against a ministry you are supposed to submit to, or because you are just a nice person who wants to help people; please do not pursue an office.

Talk to the spiritual authority in your life:

There have been too many people that have run to the internet or conferences and applied for the ordination of a fivefold title with no teaching, training, or a spiritually proven authoritative minister in their life to convey such a title. I call these people "illegal ministers." They are operating under their own self-righteous, hyper, and individualistic authority; and not the authority that Christ intended. There must be an acknowledgement of one's calling from a church body and/or recognized spiritual authority figure (this is not to say this authority needs to be famous).

Before David became king, he had to be recognized by the Prophet Samuel (1 Samuel 16:13). Before Matthias was added as an apostle it had to be recognized by the other apostles (Acts 1:12-26). Before the installation of deacons, it had to be recognized by the apostles (Acts 6:5-6). These are just a few of the many biblical examples of there being a need for a spiritual authority, whether a person or group of believers, to recognize your ministry.

Given these examples, you need to share your desire towards ordination into a fivefold office with a mature apostle, pastor, mentor, or the denomination/association that is overseeing your life. This person or entity, should not be like a friend that does not want to offend you. This is someone or an organization, that loves, knows, and challenges you to be greater in your faith. They will not be intimidated by your calling but will want to cultivate it. Share your desire for ordination to an office, and at the right time, your spiritual covering (be it an association or person) will acknowledge your calling, and ordain you.

If you become an "illegal minister" with no real spiritual authority over your life, you will just produce "fans" and not true "disciples" of the Lord Jesus Christ. People will love you, but all you can sow into their lives is rebellion and superficiality — there will be no real substance. However, should someone become a disciple of Jesus Christ while following you, it will be in spite of you and not because of your influence. Moreover, an "illegal minister" is one who may have a spiritual authority connected to their life, but they are not truly submitted. They just have an association, but not a true bond of admiration, love, and respect like Paul and Timothy or a David and Jonathan.

Follow the structure and order of your context:

Each church or spiritual authority has a different way of equipping for a fivefold office. Some may want you to shadow a fivefold minister for a few years, attend seminary or a school of ministry, and/or serve in various capacities before being ordained in said office. The point being, the process is a good thing. The Israelites had to go through the process of wandering in the desert before getting into the Promise Land, David had to go through the process of fighting Goliath and hiding out in caves before becoming the king of Israel, Jacob went through the process of running away from his brother Esau and wrestling with an angel before he became Israel, Peter went through the process of having his commitment to Jesus challenged before becoming a leader of the early Church. Some people try to avoid the process and just want the title. No, go through the process and do not despise it. God grooms you through the process before you are placed in a fivefold ministry.

* *Note to current fivefold ministers: Do not be so quick to ordain people because you feel like having spiritual sons and daughters or mentees bolsters your ministry. You need to seriously pray about, get to know, teach, and train a potential fivefold minister before you ordain and install them. Should they not have the right heart, your name will be attached to their rebellious legacy. Fortunately for Samuel, even though he anointed King Saul who disqualified himself; his name became attached to anointing ancient Israel's greatest king, David.*

Lack Of Spiritual Covering/Mentor

If you feel like you are called to be a fivefold minister but you do not have an ecclesiological body or a proven spiritual figurehead in your life, then you need to pray for God to connect you. Do not be in a rush to get a spiritual father or connect your ministry/church with a denomination/association too quickly because you will make the wrong choice out of your anxiousness because you were not directed from the inspiration of the Spirit. God is your Father, and you do have the Holy Spirit, God can still work with you because of His grace. But you need to be praying about a spiritual covering/mentor in your life, and, at the right time, God will connect you with a spiritual father/network to help establish and strengthen your ministry.

Some people resent the idea of having spiritual fathers/ covering or authoritative figures in their lives. Because in their mind they convince themselves that they have the Holy Spirit and do not need anyone else, which is true regarding salvation. However, God has designed us to submit to God and those in authority. Why? Because the greatest commandment is about loving God and our neighbors. And sometimes what God does to get us to fulfill the latter part of the great commandment, is to put what we need in another person. So then, if we are truly respectful, loving, and even submissive to that person, we get access to what we need or would like from an individual out of mutual affection and care for one another.

To put it another way, there cannot be love without **true submission**! I believe human life is valuable and robust in meaning. I love human life and therefore submit to the idea that all humans were created in the image of God and have inherent value. However, when one does not submit to that idea, they cannot truly love all human life and they begin to dehumanize others with no regard of what God thinks. And God wants for us to love Him, but He also commands us to love other people. And that is demonstrated not in emotionalism or fanciful words, but in our submission to one another.

Could the Holy Spirit have given Elisha the double portion of Elijah's anointing without him being submissive to Elijah? Of course, the Spirit could have…but God made it so that Elisha had to be mentored and submissive to Elijah, to become a greater prophet. The widow at Zarephath had to submit to Elijah's instruction of giving Elijah food instead of her hungry child, in order to be taken care of supernaturally in a famine. Naaman had to submit to Elisha's instruction to dip in the Jordan River seven times, to become healed of his leprosy. God has chosen to place some of His greatest gifts in other people so that we learn to embrace, appreciate, cherish, celebrate, and love one another.

For a more practical example, it's because a man submits to his marriage covenant that his wife grants him access to God's gift of her body in sexual intimacy. Otherwise, if the man is not committed to his marriage covenant the woman would refuse him until she felt safe and loved again. God even made it so that if you are loving and submissive to your parents, then you will have God's gift of a long life (Ephesians 6:2-3). Having a spiritual authority in your life grants you access to things you could not have gotten as quickly or not at all on your own.

Submission Makes People Feel Too Vulnerable

Now I want you to notice what I emphasized in bold in the last section, I said, "There cannot be love without **true submission!**" Meaning that when somebody is godly and truly submissive to you, then there will be mutuality and agreement between the one in submission and the one in authority. They both benefit from the relationship and want God's best for each other. However, there is such a thing as false submission. Whereas, a person is submitted to you, not because they love and respect you, but because they want to take advantage of you (E.g., Judas was never truly submitted to Jesus, there was no mutuality and agreement).

Moreover, there are some false spiritual fathers/coverings that use their power to manipulate and dominate people (E.g., many of the Pharisees in the Scripture). As a result of false spiritual authorities, some people refuse to have spiritual fathers/mentors in their life. Because to be submissive means one has to be vulnerable and nobody wants to be taken advantage of by an abusive person!

Think about this concerning a restaurant. The famished customer is submitted to the chef's expertise in cooking a nutritious and great tasting dish. In some restaurants, you do not even see the chef! You know nothing about their background or even if the chef has washed their hands. But you are trusting the chef to make something you will enjoy and that will not kill you as a result of consumption. The chef also gets a paycheck because of your submission to his/her expertise—there will be mutuality and agreement, both benefit. Sure one could argue that the customer is more authoritative because they chose to spend their money at the restaurant. But no doubt the customer is the submissive one and the chef is in authority. The chef is holding the customer's life in his/her hands. The chef could put whatever they wanted in the food, and perhaps the customer would not notice.

Likewise, when you are submitted to a spiritual father or mentor, they can dramatically alter your life, just like the chef in my example. But just because there have been false apostles, pastors, mentors, associations; and various entities of spiritual authority, God still calls us to submit to one another (Titus 3:1). So you need to choose your spiritual covering or mentor wisely. And spiritual fathers/mentors need to choose those they father/guide as well. There are no perfect spiritual fathers/mentors, just like there are no perfect spiritual children/mentees. But through prayer, and following the leadership of the Holy Spirit, God will connect the right pairing for the advancement of the kingdom.

The reason some restaurants get a five star ranking over others is that they have customer service and chefs that have a proven track record of providing the best service. Likewise, when God leads you to a spiritual father/covering/mentor, they will have a proven track record of producing the best out of their ministries, and/or spiritual children, and mentees. True spiritual fathers want the best for their spiritual children. They will want to see you excel beyond them. In other words, you do not come into your own, on your own! God always works through covenant and community. There will always be someone to help you along the way.

CHAPTER 12

APPLYING THE FIVEFOLD TO YOUR CONTEXT PART TWO

Some of you might be church leaders who are thinking about making your church fivefold. The question becomes, "How do I begin the process of becoming a fivefold church?" And what I want to say to you, is to start where you are! There is a lot of studying and growth that needs to take place before you attempt to make your church run on a fivefold government. So let me give you a few tips:

- *Start reading on the fivefold ministry.* Congratulations you have started by reading this book. Now take what you have learned from these pages and begin to look through your Bible from a fivefold lens. Where in the Bible do you see glimpses of fivefold ministry? How does the Bible itself function apostolically, prophetically, evangelistically, pastorally, and like the teacher. For example, the Bible itself is prophetic in that there are things yet to be fulfilled from Scripture. Now, how do you think the Bible is pastoral, etc? Consume articles and books on the fivefold ministry. You might need to read my book again. Get a firm grasp and understanding on fivefold ministry, and let God reveal what you need to know.

- *Visit a fivefold church.* As a church leader, you might already be preoccupied with your own service on Sunday morning. So, find a fivefold church with an evening service or on a day you are free and visit. Upon visiting make yourself known to the leadership that you are there to enjoy fellowship and learn about fivefold ministry. The church does not have to necessarily become your mentor on fivefold. But it's just best as fellow ministers to make your intentions known while visiting their church. Make sure you give an offering when you are there and that you are interested in having genuine friendship with them. It does not mean you will visit that church forever, but you should make friends with fivefold ministers. Being in the atmosphere is contagious, and it should rub off on you.

If you are not a minister, but you belong to a non-fivefold church, there is nothing wrong with visiting one. As long as your visit does not take away from your commitments to your current church. Your tithe, service, and commitment to your church should remain intact. God does call us to belong to a church. Hence, unless God has called you to another church, do not become disobedient and leave the church you belong to. And if you do sense that God is calling you to be committed to a fivefold church, please let your current church leaders know. Those church leaders love you, have prayed for you, and have grown you in your faith. God put them in place to develop your spiritual life for a season. Do not dishonor God, by dishonoring them. Let them know God is calling you elsewhere.

- *Spiritual father/mentorship.* If you do not have a spiritual father, then you need to pray about someone who can father you in the fivefold. However, you may already have a spiritual father, but you just need a mentor or a coach. Whatever the case may be, they can help you discover your office, help you understand more about the fivefold, and/or help your church transition into the fivefold ministry. You need an authoritative person in your life who understands how to guide you.

- *Be committed.* If fivefold is something you truly want, then be committed to it. There are some really good Christians who love the Lord, but have not received this revelation of the fivefold ministry. As a result, you might be ridiculed and rejected because of it. Moreover, do you have the faith? If you are still struggling to believe this topic and/or you do not believe in miracles, signs and wonders, then you are not ready to pursue this as of yet. Apostles and prophets function in the supernatural. And if you still struggle to believe in the supernatural, then you should not teach, practice, or try to implement only part of the fivefold you are willing to accept. **Embrace all of the fivefold ministry, or none of it**. Keep studying and ask God to increase your faith. And once the faith is there, then go forward in discerning your own office or how your church can operate as fivefold.

- *Humility*. The fivefold is an authoritative and biblical model of doing church. It's not like the congregationalist model, where regardless of the maturity level, each member gets a vote. No, that model often empowers the Judas of your congregation to vote, and we all know that Judas votes for his own selfish ambitions. Moreover, when the whole congregation of Israel voted for or against Jesus to die, they chose Barabbas over Jesus (John 18:38-40). I am not saying a congregation cannot be trusted, it's just wrong to assume or place the burden of leadership on the entire congregation and make them accountable before a holy God. Not everyone is at that place of leadership. There should be a true leader that willingly stands out and makes the tough decisions, so the rest can live in freedom.

Some people criticize fivefold ministry because of its authoritative sense of the visionary leader—for they make the final decision. But the reality is, whenever the whole congregation gets a vote on what God wants the church to do, it automatically produces division or a schism. Because one half of the church votes "yes" and the other half votes "no." So now the church breaks out into factions, just like the divide between republicans and democrats in the United

States, and nothing gets done in the church. Or if they do not break out into factions, then they become despondent to the mission of the church, and become passive voters because they know their vote can be cancelled out if they are in the minority.

Furthermore, the truth of the matter is that there is always one person or a small group running the entire church even if it appears to be a congregational vote. There is always the person that has given the most money, has the most family members at the church, appears to be the most talented and anointed, or has been at the church the longest that tries to have the biggest voice and turn people's votes. As much as we try to deny it, if you have been involved in church leadership for a little while, you know there is always a single visionary leadership present through an individual or a small group of affluent people.

Hence, the fivefold just points out the obvious…that the church does need a visionary leader to make final decisions if the church wants to get anything done. God does send a visionary like Abraham, Moses, Deborah, David, Solomon, John the Baptist, Paul, Peter, and the like, to galvanize people towards the will of God. The visionary fivefold leader does need the wise council of other fivefold ministers, elders, etc., it's just that it should not come from everybody. It should be wise council assisting the visionary leader to make godly decisions, like Jonathan was to David.

With this being said, one needs to have humility if they are going to be the visionary leader. In other words, hopefully one is not trying to use the fivefold to prop themselves up above people with no real intention of helping the Body of Christ mature. We should not have any worry about a visionary leader, who is called by God, and making the final decision if they are full of humility. Moreover, we have to be willing to trust God to remove a visionary leader should they become corrupted (E.g., King Saul is replaced because of his disobedience). Furthermore, even though my wife and I are the visionary leaders of our church, there are provisions in my church's by-laws towards the removal of the visionary leader from office, should the visionary become abusive and/or heretical.

The visionary leader must be full of humility and have a robust understanding of the role and responsibility of the fivefold, elders, deacons, and the congregation, so they know how to establish people in their own ministry within the church and the world. The fivefold are just good stewards of God's Church, and kingdom manifestation.

Note of caution. Please do not try to make your church fivefold without first having a full acceptance and at least an overview understanding of the function and responsibility. The aforementioned is just a list for your thoughts with no particular order in mind. Hence, you need to start with prayer. Hear God's direction for how you should go about establishing yourself and His church in the fivefold.

Two Ways Of Implementing The Fivefold

I am sure there are more ways than two, and nuances on how one goes about it. Nevertheless, these two seem to be the most prominent. So let's start with the ways of establishing a fivefold church with the easiest being first:

Church planting: This meaning that God has truly called and sent you into an area to establish a kingdom church with the fivefold as its governing rule. It's important for me to say, you only plant a new church if God is telling you to. Some people have attempted to plant churches because it was a good idea but not a God idea. Just because you have the money and people backing you, does not mean you should plant a church. However, when you are pioneering a new church you get the opportunity to establish the culture or set the atmosphere of that church.

Naturally, as you are writing the vision and sharing it with people to join you in this new endeavor, you can articulate it as a fivefold church. This does not mean on day one of your new church start, you need to have every office of the fivefold present and be able to articulate the mysteries of the kingdom with eloquence. No, just start with whatever office you are, teach what you currently know, and as you attain more revelation knowledge, make it applicable to your church with the grace God has given you— develop the fivefold culture as you personally grow. As a matter of fact, God might only be asking you to mention and broach the idea of fivefold ministry in year one or two of your church plant, without delving too much into the details and application. Because at the beginning of your church plant, God may want you to talk more about church as a family, a community, or the Bride of Christ; He might just want you to talk about traditional doctrine, salvation, and outreach projects. Why? Because at the beginning of your church plant God could just want people to gather as the family of God, with a proper understanding of who God is, and to do outreach to reach the lost. Establishing the fivefold does not need to be overt at the beginning stages of your church plant, instead it is a part of your frame work that you gradually implement.

Some of you, may already have strong knowledge of your office, and fivefold ministry as a whole. So, depending on the Lord's timing, you might start your church plant immediately with classes and Bible studies on fivefold ministry. Moreover, if you are not doing your church plant from scratch, but are being sent out by a church that is already fivefold, then it's easier because you are an extension of what your mother/ affiliate church has already done. You just might articulate the fivefold a little different based on how God has graced you. But there is already a foundation and expectation for the new church to be fivefold because of the credibility of your mother/affiliate church.

I cannot stress enough that church planting is for truly called people. There have been too many people that have started a church and then quit 18 months later...because the church did not get over thirty people fast enough. Those thirty people may have been committed and just needed a little more time to grow, but the church planter quits and leaves God's bride due to vanity. They recite a noble reason for quitting, but what they do not want to admit is that God never really called them or that their ego is too bruised to continue. In essence, they end up wasting time and God's resources that could have been used elsewhere. And yes, God may call a minister to a place for a short season. But, a lot of what is happening in today's ministry climate, is the uncalled minister quitting because they were never anointed to do it. Or the called minister quitting a church plant too early, because it became inconvenient for them. If God called you to an area, stay there until the job is truly done. God will take care of you no matter how tough it gets. Jeremiah had every reason to quit his ministry because the people to whom he was called would not even listen to him, but he fulfilled the call God had on his life. You get your head up and do likewise.

Church revitalization: A church could be relocating, new leadership is being installed, by-laws are being re-written, or a church is trying to develop new strategies for ministry. During this transition period, it could be a good time to introduce fivefold as a vital part of the church's new identity. One may be a non-denominational or independent church who has loosely believed in the supernatural manifestation of the Spirit's power, has believed in the office of apostles and prophets along with other fivefold concepts, however, they have never heard it defined until reading this book or thought about strategically implementing it into their church context until now.

The visionary leader should be able to clearly articulate why God is calling the established church towards a fivefold structure and order. Education and slow introduction is key, because the church may already be open to the fivefold, but they are used to operating in a typical non-denominational or independent style. Hence, the visionary leader should not have a dogmatic approach, but rather, a pastoral and teaching approach to begin with.

* *Denomination:* I only bring this up as an option because some of you might be thinking, "How do I get my denominational church to be fivefold?" The truth of the matter is that it is almost impossible. Could it happen? Yes! But it's very unlikely. Denominations are steeped in historic tradition. They have a long established history of how to operate a church in the way they have grown accustomed. If you are Presbyterian, Methodist, Lutheran, or some other mainline denominational stream, then church must be done their way. And to try to secretly make your church fivefold outside of their traditional offices of ministry, would just be rebellion. Either a person wants to be a part of their denominational structure or not. One could suggest to their higher ranking leadership, that the denomination should become fivefold in structure and order. But it's hard to convince an entire denomination to change their governmental strategy after years of implementation.

Visible Signs Of The Fivefold Government

When establishing a visible representation of the fivefold in a church, there is not one way this needs to look. In the following are a few visible forms of fivefold structure.

Individual offices: This is when you have recognized individuals as the house apostle, prophet, evangelist, pastor, or teacher. An individual holds that office and is responsible for overseeing and training the congregation. If there is an office vacant, it stays that way until God calls someone else into that office. And of course, there will be a visionary leader who holds at least one of the offices within the church and makes the big picture decisions.

Multiple offices within a few: The visionary leader could hold more than one office. And there is another fivefold minister on staff who also holds more than one office. Teamed together, they represent the entirety of the functions of the fivefold ministry and are graced to train the elders, deacons, and the entire congregation in their own gifting.

Collective expression: A church may only have an apostle or a pastor as the visionary leader of their church. It is the only office that is filled. Nonetheless, there are other members of the body who are not fivefold, but are matured in some of the gifts relating to an office. A deacon could have a great counseling gift like a pastor, an elder could have some strong prophetic gifting in the word of knowledge like a prophet, a congregational member could have strong outreach ideas like an evangelist. In other words, the visionary leader could employ members of the body, to lead and teach in some of these areas. They would not have the same authority and level of responsibility as a minister in a fivefold office, but God's grace would work through it. Remember, King Saul was not a prophet, but he was able to minister the prophetic when he got around prophets (1 Samuel 10:10). Likewise, there are people in the congregation that can operate, in some limited capacity, with fivefold gifts.

I believe the best and most accurate to the biblical model in Ephesians 4 of fivefold ministry is option number one. Nonetheless, one should not rush anybody into an individual office until God calls for it. One should not overly stress form over function and become religious. The form of the Old Testament atonement system was sacrificing animals. And they fell more in love with the form, than understanding its true function of pointing to the sacrificial Lamb of God—Jesus the Christ! Because the Jewish people failed to recognize Jesus as the final atoning sacrifice for sins, they rejected Him. They preferred the temporary atonement of sacrificed animals, over the permanent salvific work of Jesus Christ. They chose form over function.

One should not make the same mistake with the fivefold. Some churches may only have 10, 20, or 50 people. And as a result, they might not have all the offices fully filled. But is it any less a powerful church if it has been established by Christ? No, if Jesus is the Head of a church, it is a powerful church. So long as the structure, order, and culture of a church is fivefold, it is a fivefold church.

Closing Remarks

Having now gotten to the end of this book, I feel like there is so much more I could have said. There is more to talk about theologically, conceptually, doctrinally, pragmatically; more to talk about concerning individual offices and their function; more to talk about on how to implement the fivefold in your church—there is just more! Some which is easier said in person and more that could have been written in book form. God willing, this will not be my only book on the fivefold ministry. But this one does need to come to an end.

Much like John recognized that there was so much more that could have been written about the life of Jesus (John 21:25), I too, recognize that I am one voice out of many others, who have written about fivefold ministry—and there is even more to learn. I hope this content has deepened your understanding and in the process, hopefully brought you closer to our Lord Jesus Christ.

I am so grateful to be saved, I love the Church, and equipping and activating His Saints for ministry! The kingdom of God is an unstoppable force, always advancing, and never ceasing! To God be the glory!

ACKNOWLEDGMENTS

Thanks to my wife who spent hours looking over my content, and was a great consultant for this book.

Thanks to all the fivefold ministers and Christian leaders who have influenced me greatly in ministry.

OTHER TITLES BY BRIAN D. BEVERLY II

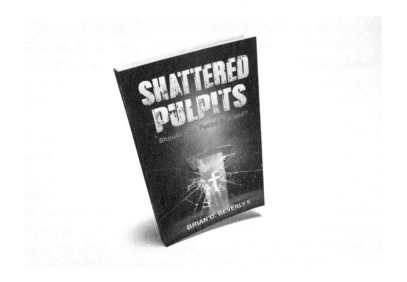

Find it on Amazon.com or brianbeverlyministries.com

ABOUT THE AUTHOR

Brian received a Master of Divinity from The University of Dubuque Theological Seminary. He also attained a Bachelor of Arts in Religious Studies with a minor in Communication from the University of Dubuque. He has been the recipient of awards for preaching and church growth. He is passionate about activating churches and people in the fivefold ministry. He is an author, conference speaker, and the lead pastor of Well of Life, in Hammond, Louisiana.

Brian can be contacted at:

Phone: (985) 318-0687

Email: Brian@brianbeverlyministries.com

Website: brianbeverlyministries.com

P.O. Box 4014
Hammond LA, 70404

Made in the USA
Coppell, TX
02 March 2020